SEAWAY TRAIL WILDGUIDE

by Donald D. Cox
Professor Emeritus of Biology
State University of New York College at Oswego

Cover Art by John A. Morrow
Illustrations by Shirley A. Peron
Special Projects Editor and Graphic Designer Kara Lynn Dunn

Published by Seaway Trail Foundation
P.O. Box 660
Sackets Harbor, NY 13685

Seaway Trail Wildguide is a collaborative project
authored by
Dr. Donald D. Cox,
Professor Emeritus of Biology,
State University of New York College at Oswego
and published by
SEAWAY TRAIL FOUNDATION
P.O. Box 660
Sackets Harbor, NY 13685
Byron C. Gale, President
Teresa H. Mitchell, Executive Director

Cover Art by John A. Morrow
Illustrations by Shirley A. Peron
and Ruth Sachidanandan
Special Projects Editor and Graphic Design
by Kara Lynn Dunn

**Library of Congress Catalog Card Number:
96-69011
ISBN: 0-943689-04-X**

The research for this guidebook was funded in part
by a Federal Highway Administration Scenic Byways grant,
administered through the New York State Department of Transportation
to Seaway Trail, Inc.

ACKNOWLEDGMENTS

It is impossible to list all the people who have been of assistance in preparing this publication. I owe thanks to the many park rangers and other park personnel, and facility managers who were helpful in providing me with information. The National Audubon Society provided Field Notes data from 1994 and 1995 for the Seaway Trail Birder's List. I am grateful to Teresa Mitchell for her positive attitude, unwavering support and encouragement, and her administrative acumen. To Kara Lynn Dunn I am grateful for her unstinting dedication to the project and her many creative editorial suggestions. I thank Mary Burdette Watkins for her encouragement in the early stages of the project. I am indebted to Lisa and Mark Lattime and Deborah and Alan Lattime for their help in collecting information from the Rochester area. I am especially grateful to Barbara Cox, Shirley Peron, and Marilyn Shapiro for reading the manuscript and offering many helpful suggestions for its improvement.

Table of Contents

INTRODUCTION

The Seaway Trail was established by the New York State Legislature in 1980. It extended from the Seaway International Bridge at Rooseveltown to the Rainbow International Bridge in Niagara Falls. In 1983 the U.S. Secretary of the Interior designated it a National Recreational Trail and it became the longest such trail in the United States to be so honored. The trail was extended to the Pennsylvania border in 1986, and across the Keystone state to the Ohio border in 1982. Today, it spans 504 miles along the American shorelines of the St. Lawrence River, Lake Ontario, the Niagara River and Lake Erie.

In addition to many recreational opportunities on land and water and learning experiences, Seaway Trail travelers enjoy great scenic beauty. The forests, fields, meadows and wetlands along the byway contribute to much of this beauty. Each of these is a natural community of living organisms carrying out the daily activities of their life cycles. These communities and many of their plant and animal members are identified and illustrated in the following pages. An understanding of these aspects of the landscape, including their composition, history, and how they are interrelated, gives an increased depth of appreciation for the diverse scenic beauty afforded by traveling the trail.

In the final chapter of this publication, natural areas along the Seaway Trail and places of regional natural history interest are located and described. These include the public beaches, state, county and municipal parks, natural history museums, zoos, botanical gardens, recreational trails, and canoe routes. We suggest calling ahead to confirm hours of availability for touring these areas and sites.

The dates given in Chapter I were provided by Suggested Reading #s15, 17 and 22. The agriculture data in Chapter II, with greater details, can be found in reading reference #23. Hunting and trapping harvest data from New York State are given in Suggested Readings #24 and #25.

Traveling NYS' Seaway Trail can be a vacation adventure and an exciting way to learn more about the fascinating natural history of the eastern Great Lakes region. Guidebooks on other aspects of the Seaway Trail experience are listed inside the back cover.

Enjoy your journey of exploration!

Chapter I

FROM MAMMOTHS TO MOTOR VEHICLES

"In wildness is the preservation of the world" - Henry David Thoreau

Imagine a land covered by a great sheet of ice, stretching at least a thousand miles east to west, a mile or more high, and extending northward toward the polar region. To visualize this is to see the land of the Seaway Trail as it was 15,000 years ago. Millions of tons of ice compressed and depressed the land surface until it was below sea level in some areas. Geologists estimate that the level of oceans many have dropped as much as 450 feet as a result of the huge quantities of snowfall compressed into continental glaciers.

Practically every landform in New York State and Pennsylvania has been influenced by the great glaciers of the past. By 15,000 years ago the ice front was retreating northward as the glacier melted. About 12,250 years ago meltwater filled the Lake Ontario Basin to a much higher level than it is today. The area traversed by the Seaway Trail was covered by the extensive glacial Lake Iroquois, which drained eastward through the Mohawk Valley.

As the melting ice uncovered the St. Lawrence Valley (12,000 years ago) Lake Iroquois was drained and the Atlantic Ocean entered the depressed areas. Seawater flowed into the Lake Ontario and Lake Champlain Basins forming a shallow inland sea called the Champlain Sea. Much of the Seaway Trail between Watertown and Massena was covered by salt water. Surface marine deposits can be observed along this part of the eastern trail as described in <u>Seaway Trail Rocks and Landscapes</u> (Suggested Readings #22).

The Champlain Sea did not fill the Lake Ontario Basin to the level of the present lake, the surface of which averages 246 feet above sea level. In fact, the southern shoreline of the Champlain Sea was probably several miles north of the current southern shoreline of Lake Ontario. Streams entering this sea continued to erode their valleys beyond the present lake shoreline. With subsequent rises of the lake level these valleys were inundated and can be observed today in such features as Irondequoit Bay near Rochester, and, farther east, Sodus Bay and Sterling Pond.

If you could be transported back to the time of the Champlain Sea, the Seaway Trail region would look quite different than it does today. First, you would notice the absence of trees. Characteristic features of the landscape would include scattered clumps of grasses and grass-like plants and other low-growing herbs, some with large brightly-colored summer flowers. In other areas, you might observe patches of mosses and lichens or thickets of dwarf birch and willow or other low shrubs. Probably none of these would exceed a height of one foot. In locations protected from the wind, you might see scattered patches of stunted black spruce and jack pine. Bare soil would be exposed on slopes where the water-saturated soil had flowed down hill.

When the glacier retreated northward it left many large chunks of ice buried in the glacial debris. By the time of the Champlain Sea, many of these ice blocks had melted causing depressions that geologists refer to as kettles. Very often these filled with water forming ponds and small lakes some of which persist today as swamps or bogs.

a mastodon

The animals you would observe in the Seaway Trail area during glacial Lake Iroquois and Champlain Sea times are quite different than the ones occupying the area today. As you might expect from the nearness of the glacier, climatic conditions were severe, with short, cool summers and long, cold winters. These conditions as well as the vegetation described earlier are similar to the Arctic tundra of today. In spite of the harsh climate a variety of animals occupied this habitat. Among these were mastodons and mammoths, both members of the elephant family, ground sloths, dire wolves, musk oxen and caribou. Two thousand years later, by 10,000 years ago, the mastodons, mammoths, ground sloths and dire wolves were extinct. To date no satisfactory explanation has been found to account for the disappearance of these animals. However, the musk oxen and caribou continued to follow the glacier as it retreated northward to the regions they occupy today.

The first humans to set foot upon what would become the Seaway Trail were people referred to by archaeologists as Paleo-Indians. There is evidence of their presence in central New York between 12,000 and 10,000 years ago. They were probably the only humans ever to gaze upon the Champlain Sea. As hunter-gatherers, living in bands of 20 to 50, they did not maintain permanent settlements but moved over large territories harvesting natural plant foods or following migrating animal herds.

Favored sites near the shores of the Champlain Sea may have been used by these people as summer hunting camps. Their hunters traveling eastward along the route of the Seaway Trail on the southern shore of Lake Ontario would have moved along a ridge. To their left the land would have sloped downward toward the north. In the distance at the bottom of a long slope they would have seen the Champlain Sea. Animals were likely attracted to the shores of the sea to lick the soil and rocks for traces of salt. Thus, the hunters may have observed herds of caribou, musk oxen, and perhaps even a mammoth. Their chief prey was probably caribou. The main hunting weapons were spears tipped with flint points, each point characterized by a groove along one side into which the spear shaft was attached with a rawhide thong. Although mammoths and, farther south at the forest margin, mastodons were apparently plentiful, there are no indications that Paleo-Indian hunters of the Northeast pursued these large animals.

a mammoth

As the ice continued to melt, the great weight of the earth's surface was relieved and the land gradually began to rebound. The rate of rise was more rapid at first then decreased over the next few thousand years. Today the Lake Ontario Basin continues to rebound but at a rate so slow that it is almost imperceptible. By about 10,000 years ago the St. Lawrence Valley was above sea level and the Champlain Sea had drained away to be replaced by an early stage of Lake Ontario. By this time the open tundra vegetation had given way to closed forests of spruce, fir and pine. The early forests of black spruce and jack pine were replaced by white spruce, balsam fir, and white pine. Evidence from fossil pollen studies suggests that as the climate warmed, white pine became the dominant tree of this forest. The route of what is now the Seaway Trail wound its way through dark evergreen forests with needle-carpeted floors.

The evergreen forest environment supported an entirely different animal population than the open tundra. The caribou and musk oxen followed the retreating glacier northward and were succeeded by moose, elk, and white tailed deer. The latter animals do not normally congregate in herds, as did the musk oxen and caribou, and they may not have been as readily killed for food. Some of the Paleo-

Indian groups followed the caribou herds northward into Canada and became the foundation for later Indian cultures in that region. The archaeological record is much less clear about the fate of the Indians that remained south of Lake Ontario. The relative scarcity of artifacts in the form of spear points and stone tools from this period suggests a rather sparse human population. The Indian cultures that later developed in this region are believed to have been established by immigrants from the south.

A warming climate allowed the seeds of evergreens, especially spruces and firs, to disperse farther north, and beginning about 8,500 years ago temperate forest trees invaded the region of the lower Great Lakes. The climate may have been warmer and more moist than it is today. White pine remained a major component of the forest joined by hemlock, oak, maple, birch, elm and ash. This forest persisted for the next 3,000 years, or until approximately 5,000 years ago, with fairly uniform climatic conditions. Toward the end of this period, climatic warming began and beech, hickory and oak increased in abundance. A traveler along the Seaway Trail during this time would have observed stately white pines, hemlocks and white oaks with straight trunks up to five feet in diameter and extending upward 30 to 50 feet before the first branch.

The warming trend reached a peak that lasted from about 5,000 to 2,000 years ago, accompanied by a decrease in available moisture. Fossil pollen studies indicate that the main influence of this warming on the forest was a significant decline in hemlock and an increase in oak, hickory and beech. There was an abundance of white oak acorns, hickory nuts and beech nuts. White oak acorns are more edible than those of other oaks because they contain fewer bitter compounds called bitter tannins. All of these are important foods, and an increase in the trees that produced them may have contributed to the northward migration of southern Indians.

One group known as the Lamoka Indians established a sizable village just to the south of eastern Lake Ontario. These were hunting-gathering-fishing people who lived in a community of several rectangular, skin or bark-covered lodges. They fished the streams and lakes, including Lake Ontario, with nets and bone hooks. Their main source of meat was probably deer, supplemented by moose, bear, beaver and wild turkey. A Lamoka hunter traveling the route of the Seaway Trail would have carried a spear with a hand-held launching stick, called an atlatl, to give him greater distance and force.

Following the long interval of warm, dry climatic conditions, a cooling trend began in central New York some 2,000 years ago. According to fossil pollen studies, this cooling has continued into modern times. Global warming resulting from the combustion of fossil fuels and other human activities may reverse this trend, but that remains to be seen. A notable influence of the cooling trend was an increase in the moisture available to plants. This resulted in the return of hemlock as a major forest tree. The cooling also brought a decrease in the proportion of drought-loving trees. The accompanying loss of food from the hickory nut crop is thought to have contributed to a decline in the Indian population in central New York.

Although there has been variation in the density of the populations, the region of the Seaway Trail has been continuously occupied by Indians for the past several thousand years. By about 1000 A.D. the Owasco culture had become established here. These were the first known people in the Northeast to practice agriculture. They planted crops of corn, beans, squashes and sunflowers, collected other wild foods, and hunted deer.

It is not surprising that an abundance of food eventually led to an increase in the size of the population with some communities reaching three to four hundred individuals. The demand for food created by a larger population resulted in competition and conflict among communities for favored hunting, fishing and crop lands. In order to defend themselves from raids by other groups, communities were forced to build heavy stockades around their villages. Warfare became a way of life and there is evidence for ritual human sacrifices and cannibalism of enemy warriors. A Seaway Trail traveler during this time would have had to keep a sharp eye for bands of fierce, painted warriors, armed with war clubs, and bows and arrows, on the way to raid or on the way home with loot and captives.

The Owasco Indians, who occupied central New York from about 1000 to 1300 A.D., were the direct ancestors of the Iroquois Indians of recent historic times. By 1400 A.D.

dire wolf

the Iroquois tradition with its palisaded villages containing as many as 700 people had replaced the Owasco culture. Like their Owasco ancestors, the Iroquois cultivated corn, beans and squashes, and supplemented their diet by hunting, fishing and collecting wild plant foods.

The main Iroquois tribes or nations south and east of Lake Ontario in central New York were Mohawk, Oneida, Onondaga, Cayuga and Seneca. Warfare and raiding among the tribes with its negative effects on the lives of people and sometimes on tribal economy continued to be a way of life. The tribes also experienced raids and warfare from Algonkian tribes to the east and north. As internal strife among the Iroquois nations intensified, they became even more vulnerable to raids from outsiders.

According to Iroquois legend, in the late 1500s, a holy man named Dekanawida had a vision in which he saw the five nations united. Dekanawida, who, according to the legend, was born of a virgin Huron maiden, admonished the tribes of the Iroquois to pursue peace and stop killing one another. A Mohawk warrior named Hiawatha, despondent over the murder of his family, became a follower of the holy man and together they travelled from tribe to tribe with their message of union and peace. After much opposition and heated discussion, the tribes agreed to join forces and initiate the League of the Five Nations. Whether or not the legend is true, by the early 1600s the Five Nations was one of the most powerful confederations of Indians in North America.

At the time when the Iroquois Confederacy was at its peak, the route of the Seaway Trail at its western end crossed the hunting grounds of the Erie Indians south of the lake that bears their name. The Erie Indians occupied what is today northwestern Pennsylvania and western New York and were not part of the Iroquois Confederacy. In fact, they were enemies of the Five Nations. As the trail continued eastward, perhaps as a hunting trail or a warriors' path, it crossed first the hunting grounds of the Seneca, then the Cayuga, then the Onondaga. As the trail turned northward following the shorelines of Lake Ontario and the St. Lawrence River, it entered the northern reaches of the Oneida territory which bordered the hunting grounds of the enemy Huron Nation on the north side of the river. Over most of its route the trail passed through deep forests of tall hemlock and white pine along with beech, sugar maple, ash and basswood.

By the middle of the 1600s faces other than Indian could be seen in the Seaway Trail region. During the 1700s Europeans began to arrive in greater numbers and by the late 1700s European-type civilization was well on its way to the lands of both the Five Nations and their Algonkian enemies.

During the 1800s and early 1900s, to supply lumber for a growing white man's society, the great stands of white pine, hemlock, beech and sugar maple were put to the axe. These were eventually replaced by impressive second and third growth forests, but the white pines never returned in the numbers that existed in pre-colonial forests.

Today the Seaway Trail is a two-lane highway that winds its way through beautiful forests, past meadows, cornfields, wetlands, cities and villages as it follows the shorelines of Lake Erie, the Niagara River, Lake Ontario and the St. Lawrence River. It is a NYS-designated Scenic Byway route which can be traveled by both motor vehicle and boat.

If you use your imagination perhaps you can see a mammoth or a herd of caribou grazing in that open field on the lakeshore stalked by a Paleo-Indian with his spear. Or perhaps with your mind's eye you can see a band of painted Iroquois warriors, the original stewards of this land, as they jog softly along a woodland path.

As you move along the trail and observe the beauty of its natural wonders, the satisfaction of knowing its past will add to the pleasure and understanding of what you see.

Chapter II

THROUGH THE SEASONS IN A FOREST

"The clearest way into the universe is through a forest wilderness"
                                                      - John Muir

The Climate for Trees

Until 200 years ago the area traversed by the Seaway Trail had been covered by unbroken forest for thousands of years. This changed with settlement by Europeans but a significant part of the trail still passes through forestland. Even when it is not passing through a forest, at no point along the trail are trees completely out of sight, even in cities. The natural vegetation of the region and the whole eastern part of North America is forest.

In order for trees to grow in any area the precipitation must be equal to or greater than the potential for evaporation. To understand this, imagine a container with a surface that allows the maximum amount of evaporation to take place. If this container is supplied with a constant source of water and it loses water in an amount equal to or less than the natural precipitation in the area, this is tree country. It is said to have a precipitation-evaporation ratio equal to or greater than one.

This is an oversimplification though because the distribution of precipitation is as important as the total amount. In some parts of the midwestern grassland there is enough precipitation in summer to support tree growth, but not enough in winter. In the shrub areas of southern California there is often enough precipitation to support tree growth in winter but not in summer. For an area to support a natural vegetation of trees the precipitation must be about 30 inches or more and be fairly evenly distributed throughout the year.

Trees can grow in temperatures ranging from 120°F in oases in the Sahara Desert to -70°F in Siberia. Thus, temperature does not seem to be a factor in determining where trees can grow. A factor that does exert a powerful influence on the northern limit for tree growth is the duration of the growing season. During the growing season trees must produce seeds and manufacture enough carbohydrates to last through the winter. It has been estimated that in order to do this the growing season must consist of at least eight weeks during which the average temperature does not drop below 50°F. If the season is shorter or the average temperature lower, there are no trees. The only places trees do not grow in the Seaway Trail region are where they are kept out by conscious human effort or where it is too wet for them.

The climatic conditions in all the counties crossed by the Seaway Trail are very favorable for tree growth with precipitation almost evenly distributed throughout the year. Oswego County, New York, near the trail's mid-section, serves as an example. In the City of Oswego temperature records have been kept for at least 88 years and precipitation records for at least 96 years. The average annual temperature is 47.3°F with a range of 47.5°F between the coldest month (January) at 23.1°F and the warmest month (July) at 70.6°F. The average monthly temperature for the summer months of June, July and August is 68°F. The average annual precipitation is 41.24 inches with a range of 1.86 inches between the wettest month of November at 4.44 inches and the driest month of July at 2.58 inches.

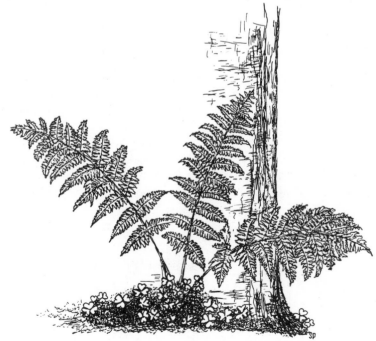

tamarack, balsam fir

The special conditions necessary for the growth of trees do not prevail everywhere. In North America there are several distinct types of vegetation, each associated with a geographical region. These include:

- the Arctic tundra in the far north, characterized by a substrate that is permanently frozen except for a shallow surface layer that thaws during summer;
- the boreal forest, or taiga, a band of coniferous trees in central and northern Canada along the southern margin of the Arctic tundra;
- the deciduous forest, covering roughly half of the United States and southern Canada;
- the prairie or grassland, mainly between the deciduous forest in the east and the Rocky Mountains in the west;
- the western coniferous forest that includes the Rocky Mountains and the Pacific coast and extends northward into Alaska; and
- the desert, mostly in the southwest United States and northwestern Mexico.

These are known as biomes and only three of them, as their names suggest, have climatic conditions that will support the growth of trees.

white spruce, black spruce

The Evergreen Forest

In the northeast there are two types of forest: deciduous and evergreen. Beginning at the Atlantic Ocean and extending across central Canada and through central Alaska to the Pacific Ocean is the largest evergreen coniferous forest in the world. It is known as the boreal forest, or taiga, and it continues in a similar band at the same latitude across Siberia and northern Europe.

The main trees making up this forest in North America are balsam fir, white spruce, black spruce, jack pine, and larch or tamarack. The combinations and proportions in which these trees occur depends on environmental conditions in that part of the forest. For example, in wet areas black spruce and larch are commonly the most abundant trees. The boreal forest is best developed in the St. Lawrence River valley area of the Seaway Trail where the main species are balsam fir and white spruce.

This forest dips into the United States in northern New England and in the northernmost parts of the upper Great Lakes.

The Summergreen Forest

South of the boreal forest in the northeast is the eastern deciduous or summergreen forest. The Seaway Trail lies in the part of the deciduous forest that ecologists refer to as the beech-maple forest. As the name implies, beech and sugar maple are usually the most abundant trees in this forest, but not the only ones. Other species of importance include red maple, yellow birch, hemlock, northern red oak, hickory, ash, and basswood.

In addition to providing an environment for the animals that live there, the beech-maple forest is of great economic value to humans. The most obvious value is as a source of lumber for construction. It is not uncommon on almost any day to see a truck of logs headed for the sawmill. Less obvious uses for individual trees include maple syrup from sugar maple, baseball bats from ash, hammer and axe handles from hickory, and veneers of cherry, and walnut for paneling and furniture.

sugar maple

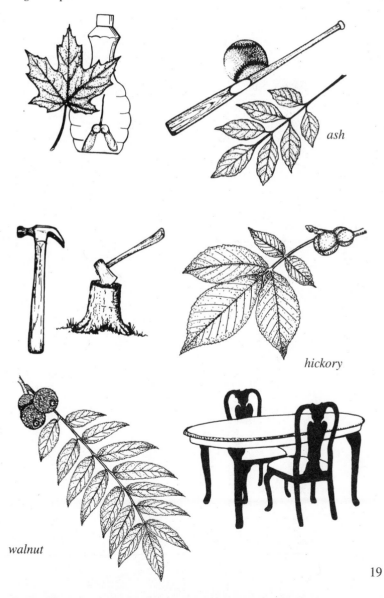

ash

hickory

walnut

The ages of a forest::
open field - shrubs - pioneer trees - climax forest

The Ages of a Forest

If nature was left to pursue its own course, undisturbed by interference from humans, all of eastern North America would be forestland. That is the way it was before Europeans arrived.

As you travel along the Seaway Trail you will observe forests in all stages of maturity. Much of the area traversed has at some time in the last 200 years been under cultivation. Before that time the route of the trail was occupied by the forests described in Chapter I. When any plot of land is cleared for crops or other human uses and then abandoned, it immediately begins to revert to forest. In the early stages you may observe a bushy field of shrubs and tree seedlings. Some trees are able to rapidly disperse seeds and establish seedlings in open fields. As time passes the tree seedlings gradually overtop and shade out the shrubs and other open field plants. Shade tolerant trees such as the ones that make up the summergreen forest are then able to become established and eventually, in the mature forest, become the most abundant trees.

This transition from open field to mature forest, called ecological succession, may require hundreds of years and the end result is referred to as climax vegetation.

From Canopy to Forest Floor

In a climax deciduous forest there are four distinct levels or layers, each of which has its own ecological significance.

The highest level is the canopy layer which covers the forest floor like a leaky umbrella. Most of the sun's rays are blocked out but raindrops penetrate readily. The upper surface of the canopy may be 120' or more above the forest floor. The trunks of canopy trees are usually widely spaced, straight, and unbranched until 20 to 50' above ground level. Shade tolerant seedlings on the forest floor grow slowly, stretching up toward the light. When a canopy tree dies or is the victim of lightning or the wind, it opens a window of light that stimulates the growth of waiting saplings that rapidly close the opening.

The canopy layer receives the direct rays of the sun and it controls the energy flow in the forest ecosystem. The environmental conditions in a mature forest are quite different from those in an adjacent open field. The forest modifies and moderates the conditions of life under the canopy. Summer studies with wildflowers have demonstrated that the temperature of the ground near their leaves does not get as high during the day or as low at night as the temperatures outside the forest.

You can judge for yourself the influence of the canopy if you walk into a forest on a hot day in mid-July. The umbrella of the canopy keeps the moisture in and reduces the movement of air. You will immediately notice a drop in the temperature. You will be walking into a place that is cool, moist, and still. There are many places along the Seaway Trail where you can enjoy this refreshing experience.

The second highest level or layer of vegetation in the climax forest is made up of secondary or understory trees. These are small trees that bump against the underside of the canopy but do not become a part of it. The light that reaches this level filters through the canopy and thus these trees are slow growing. They have a scattered distribution and their trunks are usually not larger than six to eight inches in diameter.

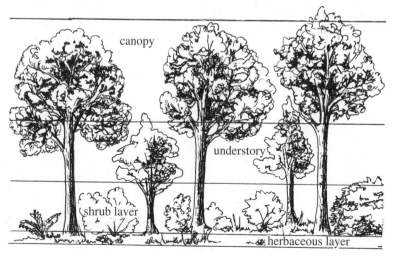

layers of the forest

hop hornbeam, sassafras,
striped maple, blue beech

Along the Seaway Trail you may observe the following trees in this layer: ironwood or hop hornbeam, sassafras, striped maple, blue beech or musclewood, some species of serviceberry, and choke cherry.

Below the understory trees in a mature forest is the shrub layer. Shrubs are woody plants that usually grow in clumps made up of a few to many stems. They may vary in height from one to more than 10'. Through millions of years of evolution they have developed characteristics that make it possible for them to grow in forest shade. They could not survive in an open field.

Some common forest shrubs you may see in the Seaway Trail region are common elder, spice bush, hobble bush, arrowwood, honeysuckle, maple-leaved viburnum, and serviceberry.

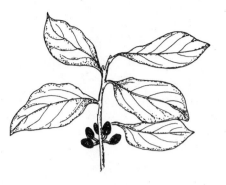

Common forest shrubs:
spicebush, elder

serviceberry

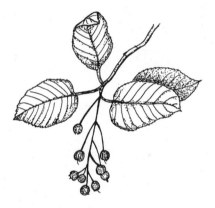

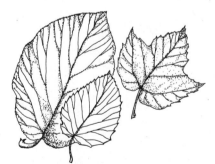

hobblebush, arrowwood,
maple-leaved viburnum

honeysuckle

The lowest layer of forest plants is the herbaceous or non-woody layer. Like the plants at the shrub level, the woodland herbaceous plants have evolved traits that contribute to their survival in an environment dominated by the canopy trees. They are often less than one foot high but some grow to a height of two or three feet. Regardless of the size of the plants in the herbaceous layer, their rate of growth, time of flowering and other aspects of their life cycles are all timed to coincide with events in the life cycles of the canopy trees. Examples of herbaceous plants are given later in this chapter.

The Ecological Seasons

An important feature of the deciduous forest that sets it apart from the boreal evergreen forest is that it has four distinct seasons. In contrast, the taiga is a constant green summer, fall, winter, and spring.

The four seasons in the forests are only loosely correlated with the calendar seasons. The latter are based on the astronomical position of the earth relative to the sun, and they divide the year into four approximately equal segments. In the forest, the seasons are marked by ecological rather than astronomical events. The canopy trees of the climax forest provide the markers for the beginning of the ecological seasons. These are the seasons to which the forest and all its living creatures respond.

Autumnal Coloration

According to the traditional calendar, autumn begins about September 22 (autumnal equinox). However, ecological autumn starts several weeks earlier. The daylight period begins to get shorter in late summer and this gives a signal to the trees of the forest. Certain chemical changes are initiated causing the trees to begin to close down their summer activities. Substances are produced that promote the onset of dormancy and the beginning of a special layer of cells called the abscission layer between the leaves and their points of attachment to the branches.

Autumn then is a very active time chemically for the canopy trees and other woody plants of the forest. As you travel along the Seaway Trail in autumn you will not be aware of this chemical activity but you will be able to see its earliest signs - the beginning of autumnal coloration. This marks the beginning of ecological autumn and it frequently occurs in late August rather than in late September.

As autumn progresses, the special layer of cells developing at the base of the leaf first interferes with, then finally cuts off entirely the supply of water to the leaf. As this is happening, the green chlorophyll pigments disintegrate revealing the orange and yellow pigments previously hidden by the chlorophyll. In the warm, sunny days and cold nights of autumn, red pigments are manufactured to augment the oranges and yellows. This is the most colorful time of the year for the woody plants of the forest as their leaves exhibit these bright colors.

This is also the most colorful time of year for some of the plants in the herbaceous layer. The blue to lavender flowers of heart-leaved aster and large-leaved aster can be observed from August to October. During the same period the bright yellow flowers of blue-stem goldenrod and the white flowers of white snakeroot add splashes of color to the forest floor.

White snakeroot is a plant of some historic interest. Its stems and leaves contain a poisonous alcohol known as tremetol. When cattle or sheep eat this plant it causes trembling, difficulty in breathing, and often death. Since the poison can become concentrated in milk before the cow shows symptoms of poisoning it can be passed on to humans. It causes a condition called "milk-sickness" that was fairly common in colonial times. Milk-sickness was a significant cause of human death in the early 1800s. The mother of Abraham Lincoln is believed to have died of this poisoning. With modern methods of processing milk the disease is rare but still possible where raw milk is provided by the family cow.

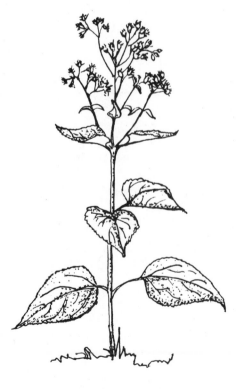

white snakeroot

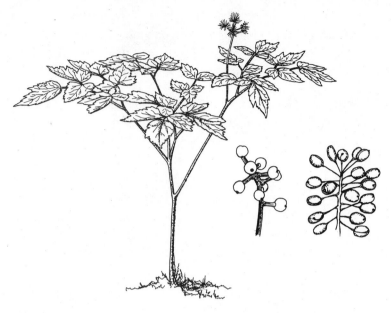

white baneberry or doll's eyes,
white baneberry berries, red baneberry berries

Other herbaceous plants produce autumn fruits that are more colorful than their flowers. For example, white baneberry or doll's eyes, in late spring, has clusters of small white flowers. In autumn it produces white berries on bright red stalks that are much more impressive than the flowers and are the reason for the name doll's eyes.

Blue cohosh is another plant with inconspicuous flowers in spring but large, showy blue fruit in autumn. Plants with bright red autumn berries include partridge berry, red baneberry, false Solomon's seal, jack-in-the-pulpit, wintergreen, and ginseng.

The Leaves Come Down

As the water supply to the leaf is cut off the cells die and the bright autumnal coloration fades. In the wind and rains of late October the leaves break away along the abscission layer that started forming in late August. Soon the trees will be bare and this signals the beginning of ecological winter.

In the forests of the northeast the leaves have fallen by about October 31. According to the calendar, winter begins on December 21 (winter solstice), but ecologically this date does not mark

Fruits of autumn:
blue cohosh berries are blue;

red berries are borne by
ginseng;

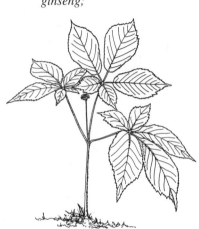

jack-in-the-pulpit;

false Solomon's seal.

27

the beginning of anything. By this time the trees are in full dormancy, hibernating animals are fast asleep, and migratory birds are already established in their southern winter quarters.

In early winter the forest is characterized by a brown carpet of dead leaves and the gray to brown skeletons of trees. Later in the season when temperatures are at their lowest, a layer of snow is likely to be present giving additional insulation to the forest floor. The result is that in a mature deciduous forest the ground seldom freezes. This is of importance for survival because the greatest threat to forest plants in winter is not low temperatures but dehydration. Winter winds may cause excessive loss of water from buds and twigs. The unfrozen soil permits the roots of trees to continue to absorb water throughout the winter. Most of the herbaceous plants of the forest survive the winter season as underground rootstocks. These also must have a constant supply of water.

The winter forests along the Seaway Trail are not entirely without color. The browns and grays are interspersed with patches of green in both the tree and herbaceous layers. At the herbaceous level, one can see the dark green, shiny leaves of wintergreen. This is a small plant seldom more than four to five inches high, occasionally still bearing a bright red berry or two that have been missed by the birds or woodland mice. When crushed, the leaves and berries smell and taste like oil of wintergreen.

wintergreen

Partridge berry is also an evergreen plant of the forest. It has a stem that trails along the ground forming mats that usually do not

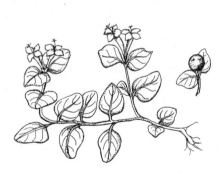

partridge berry

rise more than an inch above the ground. It can be recognized by its small, paired, roundish leaves with greenish-white veins. On the ends of branches it bears bright red berries that may persist throughout the winter if not eaten by ruffed grouse, wild turkey, or another forest dweller.

Two other plants that you may observe on the winter forest floor before it becomes covered with snow are hepatica and trailing arbutus. Hepatica leaves have three lobes thought by someone in the past to resemble the human liver, thus the name hepatica or liver leaf. The winter leaves of hepatica are reddish green and are still present when the plant blooms in spring.

hepatica

Trailing arbutus is less common than hepatica. It is a low creeping plant with oval leaves that are often heart-shaped at the base. It grows in rocky or sandy woods, and the winter leaves are usually weather-beaten and insect-damaged. Although it is protected by law, it has been extensively collected, causing it to be rare in some areas. Trailing arbutus is the floral emblem of the Canadian province of Nova Scotia and the state flower of Massachusetts.

trailing arbutus

The above plants have flowers in spring and reproduce by seeds. Some evergreen plants in the forest do not reproduce by seeds but by spores. Among those along the Seaway Trail are the clubmosses and a few evergreen ferns. Two of the most common clubmosses are ground pine or tree clubmoss and shining clubmoss. Ground pine spores are produced in a cone at the tip of the stem while in shining clubmoss spores develop in spore cases in the axils of leaves. The clubmosses are a rich green color and usually no more than six inches high. In former times they were collected extensively and even today in some areas they are threatened by collectors who use them to make holiday wreaths. They are protected by law and should not be collected for any purpose.

clubmosses

Christmas fern

Probably the most common evergreen fern you will observe in the forests along NYS' Seaway Trail is Christmas fern. It has a large rootstock from which emerges clusters of new fronds every spring. The leaves may be 17 or more inches in length and are dissected into many leaflets. The leaflets at the tip of the frond are often smaller than the others and produce spores on their undersides. According to folklore, the name Christmas fern originated because each leaflet looks like a Christmas stocking hanging on the hearth. All native ferns are protected by law and should not be collected.

Another source of color in the early winter forest is provided by witch hazel. This plant is outstanding because it flowers during what we have defined as ecological winter. Witch hazel is a large shrub that blossoms in late October, November and sometimes into December. It has clusters of bright yellow flowers with long, string-like, crinkly petals. The leaves and twigs steeped in alcohol are the source of witch hazel lotion

witch hazel

which has been described as a tonic and a healing astringent.

The drab colors of the forest's winter canopy are embellished by a sprinkling of evergreen trees. Two of the most common that can be observed in the region are white pine and hemlock.

White pine is the easiest of the pines to identify because of its long, soft needles growing in clusters of five. It may grow to a height of more than 200' with a long, straight trunk of up to six feet in basal diameter. The trees were highly valued as masts in the days of sailing ships and are still sources of strong, easily worked lumber. The white pine was one of the first trees to be harvested after settlement of northeastern North America by Europeans.

white pine

hemlock

The hemlock tree may grow to a height of 100' or more, with a straight trunk of four feet or more in basal diameter. It is easily identified by its short, flat needles that have two white lines on the undersides. In early timbering operations hemlock was not considered an important source of lumber, but was cut for the bark alone. The inner bark has a high concentration of tannin which was used in tanning leather. Hemlock bark was the main source of tannin for the tanning industries of the northeastern United States and Canada. All of the tannin used in the United States today is imported, most is derived from quebracho, a South American tree.

A virgin stand of hemlock and white pine can be observed in Hearts Content forest of the Allegheny National Forest in Warren County, Pennsylvania. This is about 60 miles southeast from the Seaway Trail at Fredonia, New York. It will give the traveler a glimpse of the magnificent forests that covered the northeast before the arrival of the Europeans.

Keeping Warm

As you look at a snow-covered forest, it may seem barren of life, but this is an illusion. Beneath the layer of dead leaves and snow, many mice, moles, voles, and shrews are carrying on their usual activities. These and other animals of the forest are going about the business of finding food and keeping warm.

Finding food is obviously a year'round problem but usually is more difficult in winter. The problem of keeping warm or avoiding cold is sometimes a bigger challenge for animals than finding food. Evolution has solved the problem in a number of ways.

Migration to a warmer climate is a survival strategy of some of the birds in the northeast. A few animals hibernate and spend the cold months in a type of suspended animation. The woodchuck grows fat eating green vegetation in summer and autumn, then sleeps the cold months away in an underground burrow. However, most of the animals that occur naturally along the trail are active throughout the year. They undergo behavioral or physical changes, or both, that help them survive the cold of winter.

Birds and mammals are warm-blooded creatures. This means that they maintain a constant body temperature regardless of the temperature of their surroundings. When the temperature is very low, they must produce enough heat by metabolism of food or stored fat to balance that lost to the environment. Conservation of energy may be essential for their survival on cold winter nights. White-footed mice that survive as solitary individuals in summer have a tendency to conserve heat by huddling together in communal nests in winter. Deer mice and several species of voles and shrews also exhibit this type of modified behavior for winter survival.

A physical change that birds are able to effect to conserve energy is to increase the thickness of their insulation by fluffing their feathers. Birds usually do not have large fat reserves so that the food they eat during the day is usually little more than enough to get them through a winter night. Some birds are able to lower their body temperature at night to reduce the amount of energy needed. Chickadees may lower their body temperature 18-22°F with a savings of 20% of the energy that would normally be needed to survive a cold winter night.

chickadee

For most mammals there is a thickening of fur with the attending increase in insulation for the winter season. In white-tailed deer, the largest wild animals likely to be seen along the Seaway Trail, there is a change in the nature of the fur and also a change in the color. The winter coat is bluish in color and is made up of long, thick, hollow hairs. There is also a tendency in white-tailed deer to show a reduction in weight in winter. This is apparently a genetically-controlled energy conservation measure since the reduced body weight requires less energy to maintain at a constant temperature.

The main winter food of white-tailed deer includes small twigs of shrubs, mosses, and the tips of cedar boughs. Walking through a winter forest you may see evidence of browsing deer in the missing tips of twigs. The preferred habitat of the white-tailed deer is not the deep woods but rather the border area between forests and open spaces.

The Bursting Buds

The shortening days of late August stimulate the leaves of trees to produce a dormancy-inducing substance. This substance may be a chemical called abscisic acid, and before the leaves are shed it is transported to the buds. Abscisic acid and perhaps other substances produced in autumn are growth inhibitors, and their presence keeps the buds from bursting into growth during warm spells in winter. Before growth can be resumed in spring the growth-inhibiting substances must be dispelled. Plant scientists are not sure of how this is accomplished, but it is known that in order to resume growth, exposure to an extended period of cold weather is required.

The length of the cold period and the degree of cooling is not known for all species, but among cultivated plants, peach trees require 400 hours and blueberry plants 800 hours of exposure to temperatures below 46°F in order to break dormancy. After the period of cold exposure, trees require increasing temperatures and increasing day length to resume growth. Most deciduous trees require a specific number of hours of warming before new growth will begin. When all of these conditions have been met, the first indication of renewed growth is a swelling, then bursting of the buds. This is the signal that dormancy is broken, and it marks the beginning of ecological spring.

trout lily

According to the traditional calendar, spring begins on or about March 21 (vernal equinox), but the trees along the Seaway Trail have not even come close to their warming requirement by this date. A more reasonable date for the swelling of the buds and the beginning of ecological spring is April 15.

Years when low temperatures persist into late April, even though length of daylight period is favorable, ecological spring may be even later. The significance to survival of this adaptation is that usually there is no burst of growth by trees during a warm spell in early spring then subsequent killing of new growth as freezing temperatures return.

The warmth generated by the direct rays of the sun plus a lengthening daylight period have the effect of an alarm clock ringing a wake-up call, not only to the trees but to the spring flowers as well. A short time later the brown leaf-strewn forest floor will be brightened by the pale blue flowers of hepatica and Canada violet, the yellow of trout lily and downy yellow violet, the deep wine-colored wild ginger, the white

mayapple

of mayapple, bloodroot, false lily-of-the-valley, and large-flowered trillium, the delicate pink of spring beauty, and the deep maroon of purple trillium and jack-in-the-pulpit. These and other flowers make spring the most colorful period on the forest floor.

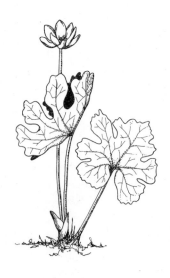

bloodroot

The same alarm clock that awakens the trees and spring flowers also awakens the early insects which pollinate and thus make it possible for the spring flowers to complete their life cycles.

The direct rays of the sun strike the forest floor in spring causing the temperature to be higher than at any other time of the year. The timing mechanisms or biological clocks of spring flowers are set for their greatest burst of growth during this period. They must accomplish two very essential activities before the leaves of the trees block the sunlight.

First, if they are to survive as a species, they must produce seeds that will become the next generation. To produce seeds, pollination must occur. Pollen is the source of the male gametes and it must be transferred to the pistil where the female sex cells are formed. Very often self-pollination will not work, and pollen from one flower must be carried to the pistil of another for viable seeds to develop. Insects are lured into performing this service by a promise of food in the form of nectar, pollen, or both. The delicate pink-striped petals of spring beauty attract bumble bees and flies for both pollen and nectar. The jack-in-the-pulpit has an unpleasant odor but it attracts beetles and flies for cross-pollination.

spring beauty

The second essential activity for spring flowers is to store enough food to last until the next spring. By the process of photosynthesis during the time that direct sunlight reaches the plant's leaves, carbohydrates are manufactured and stored in underground stems, bulbs, and rootstocks. After a brief flowering time and photosynthetic activity, many spring flowers, such as spring beauty, wild leek, dutchman's breeches, squirrel corn, and toothwort disappear from the forest until flowering time next year.

Unlike the wildflowers, most of the trees in Seaway Trail forests are wind-pollinated. Their flowers are not large and showy as are those of plants that attract insects for pollination. The wind-pollinated trees depend on air currents to carry pollen from the stamens of one to the pistils of another. This type of pollination is risky because air currents are variable and there is a chance that some flowers may not be pollinated. A survival strategy of trees in response is the production of great quantities of pollen. A large amount of surplus pollen is blown about by the wind, but it is a trade-off that assures the development of seeds and another generation of trees.

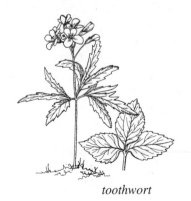

toothwort

The great quantity of wind-blown pollen is an insurance policy for the trees but it may be a source of discomfort for some humans. Although spring is not a major allergy season, some people are sensitive to tree pollen. The pollen season starts soon after the swelling of buds and is usually over before the leaves are fully developed. Trees that may be releasing pollen during this time include red maple and sugar maple, elm, beech, hickory, birch, oak, and ash. If the leaves were fully developed they would interfere with the dispersion of pollen. In response to this, evolution has set the biological clocks of these trees for pollen release before fully developed leaves appear.

Homecoming and Nestbuilding

Spring is one of the two times during the year (the other being autumn) when bird populations are at a peak along the Seaway Trail. At this time the birds that are year'round residents are joined by those that are returning from their southern wintering grounds. In addition, the area is populated by those species passing through on their way to nesting areas farther north. Great vees of honking Canada geese can be observed overhead. Some of these will stop and spend the summer, building nests and raising young in swamps and ponds along the Trail. For most of the permanent residents and summer visitors, spring is a time for mating and nest building.

Robins are often given credit for being the first harbingers of spring. In fact, most of the robin population does go south but many robins are present all winter. Some of these may be birds that have moved into the area from farther north.

Some of the most colorful of forest song birds are among those that arrive for the summer. Three that can often be observed, along with many spring wildflowers, in a moist woodlands before the canopy closes are the Baltimore oriole, rose-breasted grosbeak, and the scarlet tanager. The males of each of these species usually arrive first and are more colorful than the females. The Baltimore oriole is black and bright orange; the rose-breasted grosbeak is black and white with a red breast patch; and the scarlet tanager is bright red with black wings. These birds winter in Central or South America and are very beneficial to the summer forests. They consume many insects that are harmful to the forest and sometimes to cultivated crops as well. The rose-breasted grosbeak is particularly fond of the Colorado potato beetle and is sometimes called the potato-bug bird.

Travelers along the Seaway Trail in spring are likely to see the white-tailed deer. It is one of the most important big game animals in the United States. After a winter of feeding mainly on buds and twigs of various species, with maples, viburnums, and white cedar as favorites, in early spring deer may be observed grazing on tender young grass shoots and other herbs. In late May or early June, females give birth to their young after a gestation period of about seven months. Does commonly give birth to twins which at the age of about one month begin following the mother on her feeding route. The fawns are weaned in the fall but they usually remain with the mother through the winter.

Spring is a time of giving birth for several mammals common to the region. Raccoon females, after a gestation period of 63 days, give birth to three to seven young. The home den is often a hollow tree. Squirrels build nests in hollow trees or of interwoven leaves high in the branches of trees. After carrying their

raccoon

young for about 44 days, females give birth to two or three baby squirrels in March or April. Skunks may use abandoned woodchuck burrows or dig one of their own in which to spend the winter. (The woodchuck may have become the victim of a predator or it may have just moved to another location). After a mating season in mid-February, females give birth to four to seven young in mid-April. The female chipmunk, after carrying her young for only 31 days, gives birth to three to five babies about May 1. The young are out of the nest and above ground by June 1, and may mate in August.

squirrel

37

The Leaky Green Umbrella

Unlike the trees in a tropical forest which produce new leaves throughout the year, the deciduous trees undergo a burst of growth in spring and early summer, after which no new leaves develop. As the leaves enlarge, progressively less direct sunlight falls on the forest floor.

Imagine lying on your back in the forest looking upward. At the beginning of ecological spring you will see all blue sky. As the season advances you will see increasingly less blue until finally, when the leaves have reached maturity, you will see only green undersides of leaves. The canopy has closed to mark the beginning of ecological summer. The traditional calendar indicates that summer begins on or about June 22 (summer solstice) but closure of the canopy takes place almost a month earlier, usually about May 25.

With the closure of the canopy, there is a drop in temperature, a decrease in air movement, and an increase in humidity creating the summer forest conditions described earlier. In early summer, usually by the end of June, the buds for next spring's growth are already formed in the axils of leaves and at the tips of twigs.

The number of tree species in Seaway Trail forests is relatively low, making tree identification simpler for the amateur botanist. Methods for the identification of white pine and hemlock were given earlier. Another tree that is related to these two and may be observed, often in wet areas along the trail, is larch or tamarack. Larch differs from white pine and hemlock in that it sheds its needles in winter. The needles are soft, slender, up to one inch long, and they occur in dense clusters on very short or dwarf branches. In autumn they turn golden yellow prior to shedding, which is why the tree is sometimes called golden larch.

The forest floor in summer is not as colorful as in spring. The green leaves of many of the plants that bloom in spring persist in the deep shade of the summer forest. Among these are the ones that produce showy berries in late summer or autumn, such as blue cohosh, red baneberry, doll's eyes, jack-in-the-pulpit, and false Solomon's seal. Some of the woodland plants that may be in flower from June to August are ginseng, large-leaved and heart-leaved asters, white snakeroot, blue-stem goldenrod, spotted wintergreen, pipsissewa, and enchanter's nightshade.

Know Them By Leaf and Bark

Two patterns of leaf attachment can be observed among deciduous trees. The leaves may occur in pairs opposite one another or they may occur singly and have an alternate arrangement. Deciduous trees have two types of leaves, simple and compound. A simple leaf is one in which the blade (the broad, flat part) is in one piece. In a compound leaf, the blade is

alternate

opposite

dissected into smaller units called leaflets. To distinguish between a leaf and a leaflet there is always a bud in the axil of a true leaf.

simple   *palmately*   *pinnately*
          compound   *compound*

The leaflets of compound leaves may be arranged pinnately or palmately. When leaflets occur in pairs along a central stalk it is a pinnate arrangement. When leaflets are all attached at one central point and radiate out like fingers from the palm of a hand, it is a palmate arrangement.

The trees with opposite leaves comprise a fairly small group that includes maples, ashes, dogwoods, and horse chestnut. A convenient way to remember this is to use the first letter of the first three and the first word of the last to form the words MAD Horse. Anytime you encounter a forest tree with opposite leaves you can identify it as one of the MAD horse group. The maples and dogwoods have simple leaves, but maple leaves have lobes and dogwood leaves do not. The dogwoods are small trees or shrubs that never get large enough to be canopy trees as do the maples. The ashes and horse chestnut have compound leaves, but horse chestnut never grows wild in the forest. It is a native of Europe and Asia with compound palmate leaves and is most often observed growing along roadsides or in lawns as an ornamental. The ashes have compound pinnate leaves with five to nine leaflets.

Leaves of the MAD Horse:
  maple, ash, dogwood & horse chestnut

The largest group of tree species in the forest is made up of trees with alternate leaf arrangements. A few of these have compound leaves including walnut, hickory, and black locust. Among the trees that have simple alternate leaves are beech, basswood, birch, wild black cherry, elm, oak, and chestnut.

Although trees are most often identified by their leaves, sometimes bark or twig characteristics can be helpful. Among the canopy trees the smooth, gray bark of beech cannot be confused with any other tree. This smooth surface is so inviting that many people cannot resist the destructive temptation to carve their initials. Yellow birch bark is yellowish in color and peels off in thin sheets around the trunk. When a yellow birch twig is crushed it smells of wintergreen.

Several species of the understory trees have barks with easily identifiable features. Ironwood or hop-hornbeam has a scaly overlapping bark that resembles badly weathered roof shingles. The trunks and branches of striped maple have greenish-white vertical lines. The young stems and twigs of sassafras are bright green and have a fragrant odor when crushed. Blue beech or musclewood has a smooth bluish-gray bark and a trunk with bulges that are reminiscent of strongly muscled arms.

Plants without Chlorophyll

indian pipe

A few summer or autumn-blooming plants are unique in that they are not green. These plants are parasitic either on soil fungi or on the roots of trees. One of the most common is Indian pipe or corpse plant. It is waxy white in color, the reason for the name corpse plant, and usually grows four to six inches in height. There is very often a cluster of stems each with a single flower at its tip. At maturity the flower turns downward giving the appearance of a pipe stuck into the soil stem first. As the seed capsule ages the flower becomes erect.

Pinesap is a closely related species but it differs from Indian pipe in having tan or yellowish stems, each with several flowers. Both of these species grow in very close association with soil fungi on which they are probably parasitic. Both turn black with age.

Two plants parasitic on the roots of trees are squawroot and beech-drops. Squawroot is four to six inches high with yellowish flowers crowded on a short stem that somewhat resembles a weathered white pine cone. It is parasitic on the roots of several trees, favoring oak and hemlock. Squawroot plants are often overlooked in woodlands because their brownish color blends with fallen leaves which may partly or completely cover them.

Beech-drops is light brown to purplish in color, freely branched, and may be a foot or more in height. The dead stems commonly persist throughout the winter and into the next growing season. There is very little difference in the appearance of dead and live stems. Beech-drops is often abundant under, and parasitic on the roots of, beech trees, but damage to the host plant seems to be insignificant.

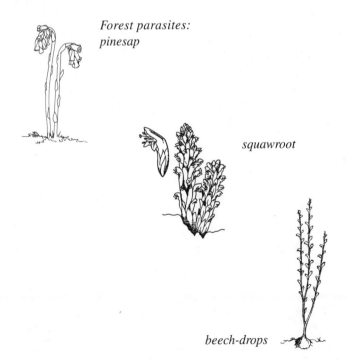

Forest parasites:
pinesap

squawroot

beech-drops

Handle with Care

Poison ivy is a woody vine most often seen in woodlands but it may grow on sand dunes, in open fields, in wet areas, or even in shady corners of your lawn. For those who are lovers of the out-of-doors, the ability to recognize this plant, with its three-parted leaf, is a must. Seventy-five to 80% of the population in the United States is allergic to poison ivy. The toxin is a colorless or milky fluid within special canals in all parts of the plant except the pollen. Humans are particularly susceptible to this toxin and at least two million people develop skin rashes from exposure each year.

For individuals sensitive to the toxin it might be helpful to review several facts about poison ivy:

• you generally do not get a reaction from simply touching the leaf or stem of the plant. The leaf or stem must be bruised or broken so that the special canals are ruptured and the toxin comes in contact with the skin,

poison ivy

• dead leaves and stems will cause a reaction as readily as green ones, and

• the plant should never be burned because the vaporized toxin and particles in the smoke may affect the eyes, nose, and lungs.

A traditional remedy for treating exposure to poison ivy is to wash in strong soap as soon as possible after contact. According to the American Medical Association Handbook of Poisonous and Injurious Plants, this is not a good idea. It takes about 10 minutes for the toxin to penetrate the skin. If a strong soap is used the natural body oils will be removed and the remaining toxin may penetrate even faster. The recommended treatment is to wash with plain running water without soap.

Another common misconception is that the fluid from poison ivy blisters will spread the rash. When the toxin from the plant penetrates the skin it combines chemically with deeper skin tissues. All of the toxin interacts with the cells so that the greater the exposure the more severe the rash. However, since all of the toxin undergoes an irreversible chemical change there is none left in the fluid of the blisters, so the rash cannot be spread when the blisters burst. There are commercial lotions that claim to protect the user in case of exposure to poison ivy toxin. For those who are allergic the best practice is to learn to recognize it and stay away from this plant.

Feathered and Furry

The crow is one of the best known birds in America. Its diet consists of practically everything edible including weed seeds, carrion, insects, eggs and the young of other birds, mice, rabbits, and in folklore it has even been accused of killing newborn lambs. In summer it is most commonly seen picking at the bodies of animals that have been killed by automobiles. Crows sometimes do damage to corn crops by pulling and eating the sprouting seeds.

crow

Although they are capable of a variety of sounds, the crow is best known for its noisy *caw caw*. It has a bad reputation, perhaps because of its unsavory and damaging food habits and its loud, coarse call. However, ecologists see it as a useful member of the ecosystem. With regard to humans it probably does more good than harm as a result of the great number of insects and weed seeds it consumes.

Two woodland game birds, the eastern ruffed grouse and the wild turkey, live in the woods along the Seaway Trail. These birds are shy and the traveler will be fortunate to see them. Although drumming of the male grouse is associated with mating, which occurs in the spring, sometimes it can be heard in summer woods. The drumming starts slowly, like a distant drum, then accelerates and ends like a drum roll. This sound is made by beating the air with the wings. When a flock of grouse is surprised it rises with a great roar of wings that is almost sure to startle the invader. When thus frightened the birds seem to fly recklessly, sometimes striking tree branches and occasionally crashing through windows of buildings. The ruffed grouse is the state bird of Pennsylvania.

ruffed grouse

The wild turkey had disappeared from New York State by the early 20th century. In recent years it has been reintroduced into the central New York area and it seems to be doing well. These birds move about in flocks of up to a dozen or more and if surprised they will first try to run away. If pursuit continues they will take to the air. The food of the wild turkey varies with the season and includes seeds, nuts, grain, and insects. Its fondness for the grain of cultivated fields and its desirability as food for humans no doubt contributed to its extinction in many parts of the northeast.

The wild turkey has been called the most grand of all America's game birds. Writing in a light vein, Benjamin Franklin stated that he favored the turkey over the bald eagle as the national emblem because the turkey was a more respectable bird.

wild turkey

During summer, as at other seasons, deer are active at all hours but are usually less active during the day. Typically they begin to feed at dusk and continue at night, especially moonlit nights, and begin to bed down at dawn. On moonless nights they are more active at dusk and at daybreak.

There are probably more deer in the northeast today than when Columbus made his voyages because deer are woodland edge feeders. The clearing of the land for crops and other uses created many more woodland borders than were present when the land was in virgin timber. In addition, the main natural predators of deer, the wolf and cougar, or mountain lion, have been eliminated in New York State. The chief predators of deer today are humans and domestic dogs. The hunting season harvest is designed to keep the size of the deer herd consistent with its natural food supply. If the hunting season harvest is too low the herd may do serious damage to orchards and crops.

In summer the old bucks travel in groups of twos or threes of which the traveler may catch a fleeting sight, as they bound across the road and into the forest. An even more rewarding sight may be that of a doe accompanied by her two fawns grazing in a field or a field margin.

Other woodland mammals that are common along the Seaway Trail but are not likely to be seen during the day are raccoons, skunks, and opossums. Each of these is an important fur trade animal. The fur is used for coats and for trimming, with skunk marketed under the trade name Alaska sable or black martin. These three animals are occasionally seen during the day and are easy to identify. The raccoon has a black masked face and a ringed tail; the skunk has a white stripe down its back and an overpowering odor; and the opossum has a rat-like nose and tail.

We have seen that the seasons identified by the traditional calendar are quite different from the ecological seasons as they occur along the Seaway Trail. A comparative summary of the two methods of recognizing the seasons is given in the accompanying table.

The calendars of the traditional and true seasons

SEASON	WINTER	SPRING	SUMMER	AUTUMN
TRADITIONAL CALENDAR				
BEGINS	Dec 21	Mar 21	June 22	Sept 21
LENGTH	90 days	93 days	93 days	90 days
ECOLOGICAL CALENDAR				
MARKER	Leaves fall	Buds swell	Canopy closes	Leaves color
BEGINS	Oct 31	Apr 15	May 25	Sept 1
AVERAGE LENGTH	166 days	40 days	99 days	60 days

*bright red partridge berries
decorate the forest's winter floor*

*after a brief flowering,
spring beauty disappears 'til next year*

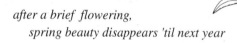

*summer shows the fruits of
jack-in-the-pulpit*

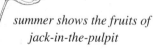

*autumn sees ginseng's
red berries*

CHAPTER III

OPEN SPACES ALONG THE WAY

"...the meadow is finished with men. Then now is the chance
for the flowers that can't stand mowers and plowers"
- Robert Frost

Open But Not Wild

The western part of the Seaway Trail through Erie County, Pennsylvania, and Chautauqua, Erie and Niagara Counties, New York, passes through great vineyards of Concord, Catawba, and Niagara grapes. Almost two-thirds of New York State's grapes are produced in these counties making New York the third largest grape grower in the United States. Many excellent and some famous wineries characterize this section of the trail.

In the 11 counties crossed by the trail (Seaway Trail Pennsylvania -1; NYS' Seaway Trail -10) about 55% of the land is cropland, hay, and pastures, 32% is woodland, and the remainder is wetlands, houses, roads, and urban development. For the traveler along the trail the most common landscape is cropland, but this does not necessarily mean open spaces because cropland includes tree crops.

Throughout its western, central, and into its northeastern segment, the trail winds through many well-tended orchards of apples, cherries, and pears. Productive orchards of Macintosh, Rome, Delicious, Cortland, and Empire apples make New York an apple taster's delight and the second largest producer of apples in the United States. New York is exceeded only by Michigan in the production of cherries and is fourth in the country in the size of the pear crop.

Since New York leads the country in production of cottage cheese, and Pennsylvania is second in ice cream production, travelers along the Seaway Trail can expect to see many rolling acres of dairy farms. Among vegetable crops, the most often seen will be fields of corn, harvested mainly as silage for dairy cows.

Other vegetable crops planted in thousands of acres along the trail are green beans, onions, cauliflower, green peas, and celery. From mid-summer to late autumn, fruits and vegetables are available in abundance from roadside stands and farm markets in all sections of the Seaway Trail.

From Field to Forest

Any cultivated field or open space in eastern United States that is abandoned or untended for a year or more is the beginning of a forest. Imagine a field in which corn has been cultivated then abandoned and left to natural growth. The first year after cultivation the field will yield a fine crop of mostly annual weeds.

An annual plant is one that completes its life cycle from seed to seed in one year and spends the winter season as a seed. Common representatives of this group are horseweed, redroot pigweed, common ragweed, wild mustard, shepherd's purse, and lamb's quarters.

illustration by Ruth Sachidanandan

48

These plants are characterized by rapid growth rates and the production of many small, often wind-carried seeds. The weeds that appear in the first year are probably there because their seeds were already present in the soil, dispersed from last year's growth of plants in adjacent areas. When they are undisturbed by plow, harrow, or herbicides they burst forth in vigorous growth.

In the second year after abandonment, biennial and perennial weeds will be observed in the field. Biennial plants are those that complete their life cycles in two years. Typically in the first year of growth they produce a dense rosette of leaves on the surface of the ground and a large taproot below. The rosette of leaves may remain green into the winter months. In the second year of growth, an erect stem bearing leaves and flowers develops and seeds are matured. This completes the life cycle and at the end of the second season the plant dies. Common open field biennials are wild carrot, burdock, common mullein, moth mullein, and evening primrose.

Plants that are perennials live for more than two years. The perennial weeds that appear in abandoned fields spend the winter as underground rootstocks that live for many years, sending up new flowering stems each spring. They also produce seeds that survive the winter and germinate in spring. This gives them a competitive advantage and the result is that they simply overwhelm the annual plants that reproduce by seeds only. Examples of common herbaceous perennials are New England aster, Canada goldenrod, brown knapweed, chicory, and milkweed.

Two or three years after a cultivated field is abandoned it will be occupied mostly by perennial weeds and grasses. Open field plants generally have relatively fast rates of growth and therefore high rates of energy expenditure. Consequently, they have high demands for light and photosynthesis and cannot tolerate shade.

wild carrot

Along with the perennial weeds and grasses, a few shrubs and tree seedlings usually become established in abandoned fields. These are slow growing plants that may not become visible for several years but eventually clumps of shrubs and individual tree seedlings will be seen protruding through the goldenrods and wild asters. Depending on the soil and water conditions the shrubs may include staghorn, smooth, or dwarf sumac, red osier dogwood, common elder, and buck-

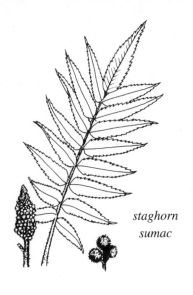

staghorn sumac

thorn. Eventually the proliferating shrubs overtop the sun-loving herbaceous plants and create enough shade to cause their elimination. At this stage the field will be occupied by a dense growth of shrubs and tree saplings.

Like the herbaceous plants these shrub populations have high light requirements and cannot survive in shade. Tree seedlings such as red maple, ash, wild black cherry, and aspen are able to become established and grow in open fields. Although they grow slower than the shrubs, they eventually overtop them. As the trees get larger and create more shade the shrubs die out and the seedlings of climax tree species such as beech, sugar maple, hemlock, and yellow birch are able to become established. These seedlings can tolerate shade and they finally become the canopy layer of the mature forest. This whole process from abandoned corn field to climax forest is called ecological succession and it may require 200 years or more for completion. The seedlings of the climax forest species are able to survive in the shade of the parent trees and if undisturbed this forest will maintain itself as long as the climatic conditions of the region prevail.

The word "weed" has been used several times and a note of explanation is in order. Weed is a human concept that usually refers to a plant growing where someone does not want it to grow. The connotation often is a plant that is troublesome or noxious. If the farmer wanted to reclaim his abandoned field he might indeed look upon the herbaceous growth as weeds. However, in the natural world, there are no weeds. As the term is used here it refers to the herbaceous plants that occur in the early stages of ecological succession.

Roadside Decorations

Markers for the seasons are less distinct in open fields than in the forest. In spring while tree buds are bursting and woodland spring flowers are blooming, the fields are beginning to turn green. During April and May, before leaves of trees have fully developed, the short-stemmed, yellow, dandelion-like flowers of coltsfoot can be seen along roadsides and in damp meadows. Large, roundish, heart-shaped leaves will appear and expand after the flowers have faded. These remain green throughout the summer and into autumn. The non-green, cone-bearing stems of field horsetail can be seen along roadsides in April followed by green, jointed stems with whorls of branches in May and June.

Also at this time, clumps and sometimes whole fields of yellow-flowered wintercress can be seen in some areas. A sharp-eyed trav-eler along the trail may be able to spot the low-growing common blue violet and woolly violet along dry roadsides. Easier to spot at this season are the white flowers of bladder campion, the stems of which may be a foot or more in height. Along damp roadsides and meadows the delicate nodding, green-edged, white flowers of snow-flake are visible in early spring.

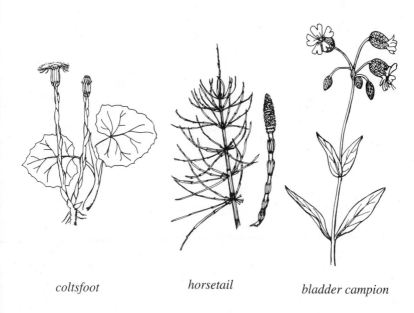

coltsfoot   *horsetail*   *bladder campion*

51

black-eyed Susan

In June and July roadsides are decorated with a variety of colorful wildflowers, sometimes seen in pure strands as strips of white, yellow, pink, or blue along each side of the road. In other places they grow in brilliant mixtures of two, three, or more colors. The plant species that make up these displays are briefly described at the end of this chapter. A few roadside shrubs also contribute to the floral exhibitions likely to be seen in June and July. These include the cone-shaped clusters of greenish flowers of staghorn sumac and the flat-topped clusters of small, white flowers of red osier dogwood and common elder.

In August and September the plants that give character to the roadsides and open fields are wild asters and goldenrods, and there are numerous species of both. The flowers of most of the goldenrods, as the name implies, are golden yellow. Among the asters the flower colors vary from white to purple. Perhaps the most beautiful of the wild asters in central New York is the New England aster with its purple-violet rays surrounding a yellow to purple center.

Each "flower" of plants in the aster family is really a flower head composed of many tiny flowers of two types. The parts that look like petals are actually complete flowers with stamens and pistils. These are called ray flowers. In the center of the flower head are disk flowers (they grow on a central disk), each with a five-lobed corolla, five stamens, and a pistil. Clustered together in dense heads, they stand a better chance of attracting insect pollinators than if the tiny flowers grew singly. Other plants in this family with similar flowers are black-eyed Susan, daisy, dandelion, chicory, goldenrod, and knapweed.

New England aster is very common along the trail and sometimes grows in spectacular roadside and field displays. For those who appreciate natural beauty it is especially pleasing to see great stretches covered with New England aster mixed with goldenrod, musk mallow, wild carrot, black-eyed Susan, and other summer wildflowers.

Contributing to the roadside colors of August and September are the fruits of some common shrubs: white of the red osier dogwood, dark blue of common elder, and the bright red of staghorn sumac.

Birds and Burrowers of the Fields

As with plants, many animal species are associated primarily with open spaces. For the bird and mammal species described here, open fields are important sites for breeding or finding food or both. The list does not include all of the animals that live in these areas along the Seaway Trail, but is a sampling of those that travelers may see. Most of the species described are year'round residents. A few are not likely to be seen in winter because they migrate or hibernate.

Eastern bluebird

EASTERN BLUEBIRD. The eastern blue-bird can often be seen near open fields in spring, summer, and early fall. The male has a blue back with a reddish-brown breast and a white belly. The female is less brilliantly colored, and the young have speckled breasts and are duller than either adult parent.

Bluebirds typically build nests near open fields or in orchards, in cavities such as a hollow branch, and abandoned woodpecker hole or a birdhouse. Each nest contains three to seven light blue eggs that are incubated for 12 to 14 days by the female. When the first brood is out of the nest the male may take charge of feeding them while the female prepares a nest for a second and sometimes a third brood.

The food of the eastern bluebird is mostly insects but they also consume wild fruits of such plants as wild grape, blackberry, staghorn sumac, and mountain ash. A characteristic behavior of the bluebird when foraging for insects is to sit on an exposed branch or fence post until it sees an insect in the grass and weeds below, swoop down on the prize, then return to its lookout perch.

In September and October the bluebird migrates southward where it spends the winter from the Ohio Valley eastward and southward to the Gulf of Mexico. Eastern bluebird populations have decreased by as much as 90% in this century as a result of habitat destruction and competition for nesting sites with English sparrows and European starlings, neither of which are native species.

The eastern bluebird is of great value to farmers because it consumes many pest insects and it seldom eats plant products grown for human consumption. It is the state bird of Missouri and New York.

EUROPEAN STARLING AND ENGLISH SPARROW. Two birds commonly seen along the Seaway Trail in open spaces and around human dwellings are European starling and English sparrow. These two birds have several things in common: both were introduced from Europe; are most commonly seen around human dwellings; are often seen in large flocks; are both year'round residents over most of the region; and are aggressive nest builders that have displaced native species such as bluebirds and swallows. Native ecosystems would have been better served if neither of these birds had been introduced into America.

The European starling is black with an iridescent greenish-purple sheen. It has a long bill that is black in winter, turning yellow in spring and summer. It was introduced into New York City in 1890 and has spread throughout the United States and southern Canada becoming a pest in many areas. The original 60 birds that were introduced have grown to a population of more than 200,000,000. Their diet includes many insects which they prefer to forage for in short grass. They also consume quantities of grain and fruits such as cherries and strawberries.

European starling

The English or house sparrow male has a black patch on its breast and is gray on the top of its head. The female is duller, does not have a black breast patch, and has a brown bill instead of black as in the male. It was first successfully introduced into Brooklyn, New York, about 1850 and by 1900 had spread throughout the U.S. and southern Canada. It was especially successful where an abundance of horse manure on the streets provided a plentiful food supply of undigested seeds. Even before it was introduced onto this continent the English sparrow had evolved a habit of living in proximity to humans and feeding on the grain and garbage they produce.

54

English sparrow

In the early 1900s the English sparrow may have been the most abundant bird species in the United States in areas occupied by humans. The populations in urban areas declined when the motor vehicle replaced the horse as a means of conveyance but the English sparrow is still abundant in farming regions. During winter it roosts in large flocks often in evergreen trees near human habitations.

RED-TAILED HAWK. There are several hawks commonly seen along the Seaway Trail. Hawks are predators with sharp talons and sharp, hooked beaks. While they usually nest in forest trees, they often forage for food in open fields. The red-tailed hawk is probably the largest common hawk. As it turns in flight it displays a reddish-brown tail and a wingspan of up to four feet. It can be seen sitting in a dead tree on the edge of a field from which it swoops to pounce on any field mouse that exposes itself.

Although its main diet consists of mice, it also takes rabbits, squirrels, and other small mammals. When these are scarce and chickens are easily and safely obtained individual hawks may get "hooked" on chickens. This is why farmers refer to the red-tailed hawk as the hen hawk. However, losses of domestic poultry to this hawk are very small.

Red-tailed hawks build large nests of sticks and twigs lined with leaves, grass, and moss. They may return to the same nest, adding to it year after year. Mating occurs and two to four brown-spotted eggs are laid usually by early May, and the female incubates them for about 28 days. Those birds in the Seaway Trail area may migrate southward in September and October to be replaced by migrants from northern Canada.

The early populations of red-tailed hawks were thinned by a bounty based on the mistaken belief that they were a serious threat to

hawk

55

domestic poultry. Their numbers continue to dwindle because of loss of habitat, eggshell thinning from insecticide, pollution, and shooting by humans.

RING-NECKED PHEASANT. This is one of the most common large birds to be seen along the Seaway Trail. It is a native of China and was introduced into the U.S. in 1887. Almost as large as chickens, these birds may weigh up to four and one-half pounds. The brilliantly colored male has a blackish-green neck with a white ring and a red face with ear tufts. He has a reddish-brown body with a very long tail while the female is brownish-gray with a shorter tail.

In the spring mating season the males fight viciously for possession of the females, and a single cock may have a harem of several chosen females. The females build their nests on the ground and incubate their eggs for about 23 days. They occasionally lay their eggs and allow them to be incubated in the nest of other large ground-nesting birds such as ducks. They produce only one brood per year with typically six to twelve young.

In fall and winter the females may stay together in flocks of up to 30. In each flock peace is maintained by a well-developed peck order in which each hen knows who she can dominate and by whom she can be

ring-necked pheasant

dominated. The food of these birds consists mostly of vegetable matter but they devour great numbers of insects as well. They are particularly fond of seed and grain and sometimes damage corn and wheat crops.

The ring-necked pheasant is a year'round resident here and a very important game bird. Since 1984 there has been an average of about 179,000 birds per year taken by hunters in New York State. These birds are relatively unafraid of humans and can sometimes be seen on roadsides or crossing the road in open or sparsely wooded areas.

EASTERN COTTONTAIL RABBIT.
The eastern cottontail rabbit is
common throughout most of the
11-county area of the Seaway
Trail. It usually does not linger
in mature forests but prefers forest margins, brushy areas, and
overgrown fields. There are probably more habitats available to

the cottontail in New York State today than when the Pilgrims landed.

It is most active at night and most readily seen just after sundown or just before sunrise. It spends the day sleeping in a scratched-
out depression under a brush pile or in a briar thicket unless flushed
from its hiding place by one of its many enemies. The cottontail is a
very shy animal with speed as its only defense.

The summer food of the eastern cottontail consists of a variety of
vegetation types, mainly grasses and broad-leaved herbs. When it is
feeding, the rabbit swallows quickly and then returns to the safety of
its hiding place. Later it defecates soft green pellets of incompletely
digested plant material which are eaten in a more leisurely manner.
During winter the main food of the eastern cottontail is the bark and
buds of small trees and shrubs.

Cottontails begin to mate in early spring and the females may
produce two or three litters of four to seven young before the end of
summer. A nest is formed by digging out a shallow depression, lining it with grass and leaves and an inner lining of fur which the female removes from her underside. The young are born about 30 days
after mating and remain covered in the nest for about two weeks. The
mother visits the nest twice daily at dawn and dusk, uncovers the
nest and allows the young to suckle. At the end of two weeks the
young rabbits leave the nest but do not breed until the following spring.

A considerable amount of damage may be done by cottontails to
farm crops, gardens, and young trees. Their chief natural enemies
are the fox and the great horned owl, but humans may be their greatest predators. If the number harvested is used as an indicator, the
cottontail is the most important game animal in the eastern United
States. In a recent hunting season the number taken by hunters in
New York State for sport, food, and fur was more than 800,000.

The flesh of the cottontail is very edible but it should always be thoroughly cooked because it sometimes carries the bacterium that causes tularemia, a disease that can be fatal to humans. The fur is not highly valued but is used in the manufacture of felt hats, for lining gloves, and as trimming on clothes.

RED AND GREY FOXES. The red fox ranges over the entire area traversed by the Seaway Trail. Ecologists believe that the red fox in eastern North America descended from the European red fox that was introduced about 1750 by colonial aristocracy for sport hunting. It has several color variations but usually is reddish-yellow or golden brown with a darker area down the middle of its back, a long, bushy, white-tipped tail, and black feet.

It occupies a variety of habitats, but often hunts for mice in meadows and abandoned fields and frequently has a den in an open field. Sometimes the den is a remodeled woodchuck burrow. Mating takes place in January or February and four to 10 young are born about 51 days later. At the age of four to five weeks, the young foxes may emerge to play around the mouth of the den. In August when the offspring are about five months old family ties are broken and the young foxes seek their own hunting grounds. They mate the following January or February. They are active throughout the year and have a life span of up to 15 years.

The red fox is most active at night but it is not uncommon for them to forage for prey during the day. Their food consists of a variety of animal and vegetable matter but they are champion mousers with excellent eyesight and hearing. It is a treat to watch a fox creep up, cat-like, while eying intently a spot in the grass, then take a little hop and come down directly on the spot where the unfortunate mouse is hiding. They also eat rabbits, woodchucks, birds, and are not adverse to a meal of domestic poultry when it is readily available. Like the fox in the Aesops Fable of the fox and the grapes, the red fox is intelligent and it likes wild grapes as well as wild cherries, apples, and berries.

fox kits at play

One color variation of the red fox is a dark coat frosted with white hairs known popularly as silver fox. At one time these were highly valued for their fur and were raised commercially. Today the value of a red fox pelt is sufficient to encourage a substantial harvest. In a recent trapping season approximately 14,600 red foxes were taken by hunters and trappers in New York State. Although this animal occasionally eats a chicken, it more than pays for this with the large number of animals it eats that would be more harmful to the farmer, such as rabbits, mice, and other rodents.

In many ways the gray fox is similar to the red fox but the former frequents woody areas more commonly than open spaces. Unlike the red fox the gray fox when pursued by dogs may climb a tree after a short chase. The gray fox is probably less abundant in the area of the Seaway Trail and the quality of its fur is less than that of the red fox. In a recent year approximately 13,800 gray fox pelts were taken by hunters and trappers in New York State.

woodchuck

WOODCHUCK. Seaway Trail travelers in summer are almost certain to see woodchucks or groundhogs. These are rather large animals that may weigh six to 12 pounds as adults. They have gray-brown fur and a relatively short, furry tail. Woodchucks are most active in the early morning and late afternoon during summer but they forage at mid-day in spring and autumn. Their food consists almost entirely of plants with which they gorge themselves all summer and become very fat. They are great diggers and their burrows can always be recognized by the mound of earth at the "front door." The burrow may be up to 40' in length and five feet underground with a concealed back entrance and sometimes a side entrance. At least one chamber of the burrow has a blind end where a nest of grass is located.

Usually by the end of October the woodchuck has retired to its nest where its large reserves of fat sustain it through a long period of hibernation. It emerges in February or March and mates. After a period of about four weeks, two to eight young are born which nurse for about five weeks. By early June the young are ready to leave the nest and establish their own burrows. They may breed as yearlings or two-year-olds.

Woodchucks may cause damage to crops and the hidden burrows may endanger horses, cattle, or people who inadvertently step in them. However, the burrows loosen and aerate the soil with a reported 1,600,000 tons of soil turned over each year in New York State alone. The burrows also permit water to enter the soil and when abandoned they provide a refuge for rabbits, foxes, opossums, and skunks.

The fur of the woodchuck is considered to be of very low value but the flesh is eaten by some people. Perhaps for their fur or because of their nuisance value to gardeners and farmers, about 700,000 were taken by hunters and trappers in New York State in a recent year.

"Groundhog Day" is February 2 and according to the legend, if the groundhog sees his shadow there will be six more weeks of winter. This is a fascinating myth but along the Seaway Trail it is almost a sure bet that there will be at least six more weeks of winter after February 2, whether or not the groundhog sees its shadow.

The Sneezin' Season

There are three periods during the year when Seaway Trail travelers, if they are among the 15 million Americans who suffer from hay fever, may experience discomfort. The first has already been described as the time in early spring when the wind-pollinated trees are producing their pollen. These include 60-80% of the forest trees along the trail. Usually this is the least severe of the pollen allergy periods. The other two are associated with plants that are commonly found in open fields.

Next in severity is the period that occurs in early to mid-summer and is associated with the flowering time of grasses. The flowers of grasses are so inconspicuous that, for most people, they would not even by recognized as flowers. Roses, however, are very conspicuous and bloom at about the same time as the grasses. For this reason allergic reactions at this time of year are sometimes incorrectly referred to as "rose fever." This is a misnomer because roses are pollinated by insects and very few of their pollen grains get into the air.

The most severe hay fever season, and the one that affects the greatest number of people, is in August and September when the common ragweed is blooming. Like most wind-pollinated plants, the flowers of common ragweed are inconspicuous. The female flowers are in the axils of leaves and produce seeds that are eaten by many species of birds and mammals. The male flowers are virtual pollen factories in spikes up to six inches long at the tips of stems and branches.

There are two species of ragweed and both are prolific pollen producers. Giant ragweed grows mostly on moist bottomlands, but the more abundant common ragweed grows in any open space including roadsides, abandoned fields, construction sites, and waste spaces. Giant ragweed, as the name suggests, is much taller than the common ragweed and has large, three-lobed leaves that grow in pairs. The smaller common ragweed has finely dissected leaves that grow in pairs on the lower part of the stem and singly on the upper part.

Goldenrod has showy flowers that bloom at the same time and very often in the same area as the common ragweed. Goldenrod is thus often given the blame for being an allergy-causing plant. Actually, ragweed produces so much pollen that everything in its vicinity, including the flowers of goldenrod, are dusted. Consequently, when an allergy victim thinks he or she is getting a reaction from goldenrod it is probably from the ragweed pollen that has lodged there. Goldenrod is insect-pollinated and does not release enough pollen into the air to be a serious allergen.

Aliens But Not Strangers

goldenrod

Although most of the plants along the Seaway Trail are native species that have been here for thousands of years, a surprising number were not here when the Pilgrims landed in Massachusetts. It may be that as many as 20% of the seed plants in northeastern United States and adjacent Canada are not native species. Most of these grow in open fields. Some of them were deliberately brought to North America as ornamentals or for herb gardens, then escaped cultivation, but most were introduced accidently through commerce and world travel. Many have been here so long that they appear to be natural residents of native ecosystems and are said to be naturalized.

tall buttercup

A considerable number of the introduced species add beauty to fields and roadsides with their colorful flowers. Among these are the tall buttercup, chicory, creeping bellflower, brown knapweed, musk mallow, wild carrot, bouncing bet, and ox-eye daisy. These species do not appear to be harmful to native ecosystems.

Other introduced species seen along the trail are not so harmless and are often noxious weeds. These include giant hogweed, Japanese knotweed, purple loosestrife, and phragmites or reed.

Giant hogweed can be observed along stream banks, roadside ditches, and waste areas in central New York. It may be the largest herbaceous plant in the northeast with leaves up to five feet wide and a stem that sometimes reaches a height of 14'. Some people are very allergic to this plant. When these individuals come into contact with the juice of the plant, then are exposed to sunlight, painful blisters and discoloration of the skin result. Introduced from Europe, this plant is very difficult to eradicate and it appears to be spreading.

Another large weedy plant is Japanese knotweed, also known as Mexican bamboo. This plant, a native of Japan, forms dense thickets and grows to a height of 10'. It has large, oval-shaped leaves and small, white, late summer-blooming flowers. It can take over a large area in a short period of time and is very difficult to eradicate. This plant can be observed along the trail on moist roadsides, in neglected yards and gardens, and in waste places. On the positive side, it is edible at early stages in its growth. The young shoots, to one foot high, can be cooked like asparagus, and slightly older stems can be used as a substitute for rhubarb-like jam. The young rootstock can be cooked as a vegetable. An effective control measure for this plant may be to serve it for dinner.

Phragmites or reed is more commonly a wetland plant but is often seen in ditches and wet roadsides along the Seaway Trail. A native of Eurasia, it grows in dense stands and may reach a height of 12 to 15'. It is a member of the grass family with broad, blade-like leaves.

Its flowers are produced July to September, in large, bushy clumps at the top of the plant. These persist throughout the year and are sometimes used in dry flower arrangements. It spreads aggressively by horizontal stems that grow along the surface of the ground. It is a disruptive factor for native ecosystems because it does not provide the food or habitat given by native plant species.

Purple loosestrife is also a wetland plant commonly seen on wet roadsides and in ditches. It has clusters of pink to red-purple flowers that brighten roadsides from mid-summer to early autumn. A native of Europe and in spite of its beautiful flowers, purple loosestrife is a nuisance species in North American wetlands. Like phragmites, it is highly disruptive of native ecosystems because it displaces native species without performing their function in the food chain.

Other introduced species of open fields frequently considered pests are dandelion, burdock, and poison hemlock. Dandelion is a native of Eurasia and a special nuisance for those who strive for weed-free lawns. A field of dandelions in flower, while it may make the farmer unhappy, is a spectacular sight sometimes seen in spring.

Burdock, a native of Europe, may grow to five feet in height and produces prickly burs that attach themselves to the clothing of any passerby who touches them. It is a biennial member of the aster family. According to mythology the burdocks were named as her own by Venus, the Roman goddess of natural productivity. The legend contends that by holding the leaves and seeds of these plants to her naval a pregnant woman can prevent a miscarriage.

Poison hemlock is a native plant of Europe and is a deadly poisonous plant. The flowers and leaves somewhat resemble those of wild carrot except that they are smooth while the stems and leaves of wild carrot are covered with fine hairs. An extract of the leaves was used in ancient Greece for the execution of condemned criminals. The Greek philosopher Socrates was so executed for corrupting the youth of ancient Athens. The poison causes death by paralysis of the respiratory system.

Another category of non-native plants that can be observed in the fields along the Seaway Trail are those that do not have particularly showy flowers and are not usually obnoxious weed pests. Included in this category are white and yellow sweet clover, teasel, plantain, lamb's quarters, mullein, heal-all, and ground ivy. Most of these were introduced into North America from Europe and Asia.

Washerwomen and Queens Lace

The following are brief descriptions of some of the most common wildflowers that can be seen in fields and dry roadsides along the Seaway Trail from April to September. Sometimes these grow in great colorful mixtures and sometimes in pure strands of pink, blue, yellow or white that may extend for hundreds of yards along each side of the road.

BIRDSFOOT TREFOIL: Flowering time: June-September; flowers: bright yellow, pea-like, in clusters at the ends of branches; leaves: pinnately compound with 3 terminal and 2 basal leaflets; shoots 6-12" high; plant introduced from Europe. The dried seed pods at the tips of stems give the appearance of a bird's leg and toes, thus the name. This is a valuable food plant for both domestic livestock and wildlife species. It is a legume with nitrogen-fixing nodules on its roots which increases soil fertility.

 BLACK-EYED SUSAN: Flowering time: June-October; flowers: heads with yellow rays and dome-shaped purplish-brown centers; stems bristly-hairy usually 1-2' high. The dead stems with seed-bearing flower centers may persist into the winter months. Eating this plant in quantities may cause illness in livestock. It is the state flower of Maryland.

BLADDER CAMPION: Flowering time: April- September; flowers: white with 5 deeply-lobed petals; sepals forming a swollen and bladder-like tube at the base of the flower; stems sometimes sprawling at the base, 10-20" high. It is a native of Europe; illustration p. 51.

BOUNCING BET OR SOAPWORT: Flowering time: July-September; flowers: pink to white, in crowded clusters at tip of stem, fragrant, with 5 notched petals; leaves: grow in pairs, each with 3-5 prominent, lengthwise ribs; stems to 2' high. When the wet flowers are rubbed between the hands soap-like suds are formed, thus the name soapwort. Washerwomen of yore were referred to as bouncing bets. This plant is a native of Europe.

Brown Knapweed: Flowering time: June-September; flowers: heads rose-purple, often more than 1" wide; leaves: narrow, toothed or shallowly-lobed; usually 1-2' high. This plant is a native of Europe and is sometimes a troublesome weed in cultivated land.

Spotted Knapweed: Very similar to Brown Knapweed but leaves are deeply, pinnately divided.

spotted knapweed, brown knapweed

Butter-and-eggs: Flowering time: June-October; flowers: yellow, 2-lipped, upper lip with orange palate, a long spur projecting from the base of the flower; flowers numerous in a long, crowded cluster at the tip of the stem; stems often a foot or more high, a native of Europe.

Canada Anemone: Flowering time: May-August; flowers: white, to 1 1/2" wide, on long stalks, with 5 unequal petals; leaves: upper a single pair, lower ones in a whorl of three, deeply parted; plant often one foot or more in height. The anemones are reported as poisonous in several publications but the rootstock of this native species is supposed to have been used in a treatment for wounds by some tribes of American Indians.

Chicory: Flowering time: July-October; flowers: heads periwinkle blue with rays square-tipped and fringed, occurring on the upper part of the stem; stems to 3' high, often with very small leaves on the upper part. This native of Europe is cultivated in some areas for its root which, when dried and ground, is used as a coffee substitute or additive.

CREEPING BELLFLOWER: Flowering time: July-September; flowers: blue, to 1 1/2" long, often in one-sided clusters at the tip of the stem, bell-shaped, hanging downward, with 5 sharp lobes; stems usually 2-3' high. This plant was introduced from Europe as an ornamental in flower gardens but is now more often seen along roadsides and in open fields.

EVERLASTING PEA: Flowering time: June-September; flowers: purple, pink or white, in a cluster of 4-10 on a long stalk; leaves: pinnately compound with a single pair of leaflets and a branched tendril; stems flattened into a thin wing, sprawling on the ground or climbing; introduced from Europe probably as an ornamental but it has escaped widely to roadsides and other open spaces.

GOLDENROD: Flowering time: late July-October; flowers: heads small, numerous, with yellow rays; plants usually 3-4' tall with narrow leaves that taper on each end. There are many native species of goldenrods. One of the most common along the Seaway Trail is Canada goldenrod, often characterized by a swollen area, or gall, on the stem caused by a parasitic gall fly. See illustration on p. 61.

MUSK MALLOW: Flowering time: June-October; flowers: 2" wide, pink or white, with 5 slightly-notched petals; leaves: lower 5-lobed, upper deeply palmately dissected; stems up to 2' tall. This European native is a relative of Marsh Mallow, another European native which is the original source of the mucilaginous base for commercial marshmallow.

NEW ENGLAND ASTER: Flowering time: August- October; flowers: heads with purple-violet rays and yellow centers; plants usually 3-4' tall with many branches near the top; leaves: lance-shaped, appearing to clasp the stem. This is one of the most colorful native wildflowers of late summer and fall and is sometimes planted as an ornamental in flower gardens.

ORANGE DAY-LILY: Flowering time: June-August; flowers: orange, funnel-shaped, with 6 backward-curving petals, in a cluster at tip of a leafless stalk; leaves: arise from ground, grass-like, about 1" wide. Each showy flower opens for a single day, then wilts. Introduced from Europe as an ornamental, this plant has escaped widely to roadsides and field margins. Flower buds and newly-expanded flowers can be batter dipped and fried as fritters.

YELLOW DAY-LILY: Similar to Orange Day Lily but with fragrant, yellow flowers.

OX-EYE DAISY: Flowering time: June-September; flowers: heads with white rays and yellow centers; leaves: dark green, pinnately lobed or coarsely toothed. This European native may become established as a weed in cultivated fields. It has been declared a noxious weed in the seed laws of nine northeastern states. When eaten by cattle these plants give an unpleasant flavor to milk. The name daisy can be traced through ancient English to "days-eye" referring to the bright yellow center of the flower.

SPOTTED TOUCH-ME-NOT OR JEWELWEED: Flowering time: June-September; flowers: orange with reddish-brown spots, with an inflated throat and slender, curled tube extending from the base, flowers dangle by slender stalks from the axils of leaves; stems: thick and soft, to 5' tall; grows along swamp and pond margins, and in roadside ditches. Mature seed pods explode when touched, flinging seeds outward. The seeds are tasty snacks with the flavor of butternuts. When the plant is immersed and pulled through the water, tiny pockets of air are trapped giving leaves a jeweled appearance, thus the name jewelweed.

PALE TOUCH-ME-NOT: Very similar to Spotted Touch-me-not but with pale yellow flowers.

TALL BUTTERCUP: Flowering time: May-September; flowers: bright yellow, with 5 shiny petals, leaves: lower palmately divided into 3-7 deep lobes; stem usually 1-3' high. As a result of its bitter juice, this native of Europe is usually not grazed by livestock and often spreads freely in pastures and meadows. Cows that eat the plant, when no other forage is available, produce unpalatable, sometimes reddish, milk. See illustration on p. 62.

VETCH: Flowering time: May-September; flowers: blue or white, in long, crowded, one-sided clusters of 10-30; leaves: pinnately compound with 5-10 pairs of leaflets and a branched tendril at the tip; stems trailing over the ground, to 3' long. This legume was introduced from Europe as a forage crop for cattle but has escaped widely to roadsides and abandoned fields.

tufted vetch

TUFTED VETCH OR COW VETCH: Very similar to Vetch but is a native plant with all blue flowers.

CROWN VETCH: Flowering time: June-September; flowers: pink and white in globular clusters on long stalks; leaves: pinnately compound with 5-12 pair of leaflets; stems spreading over the ground forming mats. This European native is a legume that is often planted along roadsides by highway departments to stabilize and enrich the soil.

WHITE SWEET CLOVER: Flowering time: May-October; flowers: small, white, in long clusters arising from the axils of leaves; leaves: compound with 3 leaflets, fragrant when dried or crushed; stems often 4-5' tall. This legume, introduced from Europe, and is sometimes sown as pasture forage for cattle.

YELLOW SWEET CLOVER: Very similar to White Sweet Clover but with yellow flowers.

WILD CARROT OR QUEEN ANNE'S LACE: Flowering time: May-October; flowers: white, tiny, in a flat-topped cluster often with one central purple flower; leaves: pinnately dissected into fine segments; stem usually 2-3' tall, a native of Europe. The cultivated carrot is a variety of this species. See illustration on p. 49.

WILD GERANIUM: Flowering time: April-June; flowers: rose-pink to purple, several in clusters at the tips of stems, about 1 1/2" wide, 5 petals; fruit with a long, pointed beak; a single pair of stem leaves, deeply 5-parted, similar leaves arising on long stalks from the base of the plant; stems usually 1-2' high. This is one of the most attractive of the spring flowers.

wild geranium

Chapter IV

WETLAND TREASURES

*"One swallow does not make a spring, but one skein of geese,
cleaving the murk of a March thaw, is the spring"*
- Aldo Leopold

What is a Wetland?

The Seaway Trail passes through, over, or near many streams, ponds, lakes, swamps, and bogs, all of which are associated with or qualify as wetlands. These are areas in which the ground is saturated with or covered by water for most of the year. They are transition zones between dry land and open water that support a distinctive type of vegetation. Often looked upon as wastelands or areas of no value, wetlands have been ditched, drained, and filled to make way for roads, housing projects, shopping centers, and other construction. From the time of the early colonists to the mid-1970's as much as one-half or more of the wetland natural heritage of the United States was lost. Since that time federal and state laws have slowed, but not stopped, the destruction of this precious resource.

A great variety of names have been applied to fresh water wetlands including swamp, bog, marsh, fen, mire, wet meadow, moor, bottomland, muskeg, and slough. The differences among some of these are slight and some refer to regional wetlands. For example, muskegs are large expanses of shallow bogs in northern Canada and Alaska.

As the many names indicate, there are a variety of types and this makes it difficult to formulate a legal definition of a wetland. In framing the Wetlands Act in New York State, legislators grappled with this problem and finally, after several meetings with professional ecologists and botanists, defined a wetland by the plants growing there. In New York State a wetland so defined, and with a size of 12 or more acres, cannot be filled, drained, or otherwise altered without the approval of the Department of Environmental Conservation.

In this chapter, to simplify terminology, two types of wetlands will be recognized: swamps and bogs. The basic physical difference between the two is in the nature of the underlying base of substrate. Swamps have mineral soil as a base; bogs have an organic or peat substrate. Swamps usually have a stream flowing through them or are drained by a stream and they are flushed annually by high water. Bogs form mostly in depressions that have no outlet and thus are not drained. Both swamps and bogs are inhabited by populations of plants and animals that have evolved special characteristics for survival in these unique habitats.

What Good are They?

Ecologists have long recognized the value of wetlands but it was not until the 1970's that legislators began to pass protective laws. Destruction of wetlands is still taking place but the process has been slowed by the passage of legislation such as the New York State Wetlands Act of 1975. The values of wetlands described here apply not only to the area spanned by the Seaway Trail but to wetlands wherever they occur throughout North America and the world.

illustration by Ruth Sachidanandan

One of their great values is the role wetlands play in flood prevention. These areas are depressions that serve as catchbasins in times of heavy precipitation. Upstream wetlands catch and hold the runoff, thus reducing the level of the peak flood stage and the accompanying flood damage. Investigators have found that the greater the acreage of wetlands along the course of a stream the less severe the flooding in times of excessive precipitation.

Another major value of wetlands is that they serve as reservoirs for the underground water supply. If you dug into the ground at any point along the Seaway Trail you would eventually reach the groundwater zone. Many rural homes, towns, and cities sink wells into this zone for their drinking water. The source of this underground supply is water that has percolated down from the surface. During extended periods of low rainfall the groundwater level drops and wells may go dry. In such times, percolating water from some wetlands may reduce the amount of drop in groundwater levels.

Perhaps the most important value of wetlands is that they provide unique environmental conditions for living things. Many species of plants, mammals, birds, and reptiles depend on this type of habitat for survival. As a consequence of habitat destruction a disproportionately large percentage of those species are threatened and endangered. For example, of all of the threatened or endangered species in the United States, 3% of the plants, 15% of the mammals, 31% of the birds, and 31% of the reptiles are associated with wetlands.

Swamps

The wetlands most often seen by travelers along the Seaway Trail are swamps. These are of two types: those which include woody plants such as buttonbush and willow, and those, called marshes, which consist entirely of herbaceous plants. Woody swamps are probably most common, but where the trail comes close to some Lake Erie and Lake Ontario embayments great expanses of cattail marshes can be seen. Both woody swamps and marshes are developmental stages that probably started in open water. Most ecologists think that these areas in the eastern United States, if left to natural forces, will, like abandoned fields, eventually become forests. The process of becoming a forest usually begins in open water and the first indicators are floating plants.

Floating Plants

American lotus

Floating plants are of two types: those that are free floating, and others that are attached to the bottom by long stems. The free-floating plants are mostly duck-weeds, the world's smallest flowering plants. They rarely have flowers, but even when they do, the structures would not be recognizable by most people as flowers. These plants reproduce asexually by producing buds on one end that detach and grow into new plants.

There are three types of duckweeds. Greater duckweed is the largest and can be recognized by a cluster of two to 16 roots that hang from the underside. Lesser duckweed is slightly smaller and has a single hanging root. Watermeal, the smallest, is about 1/25 of an inch in diameter and has no roots. The duckweeds grow on quiet waters and are eaten by ducks and other waterfowl and sometimes other animals such as muskrats and painted turtles.

Another floating plant often growing with duckweeds is mosquito fern. This small delicate fern is 1/5 to 2/5 of an inch in diameter and is usually reddish in color or darker green than duckweed.

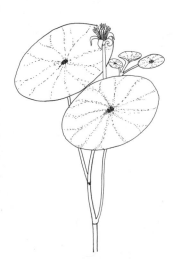

Other floating plants attach to the bottom and have floating leaves with long stems. These include the American lotus, spatterdock, water-shield, and water lily. Each of these has a large, showy flower on a long stalk that either allows it to float on the water or holds it above the surface.

water-shield

73

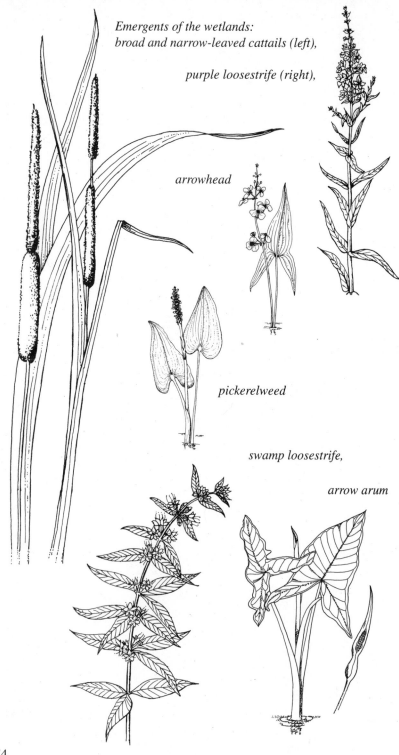

Emergents of the wetlands:
broad and narrow-leaved cattails (left),

purple loosestrife (right),

arrowhead

pickerelweed

swamp loosestrife,

arrow arum

Submergents

elodea,
hornwort,
curly pondweed

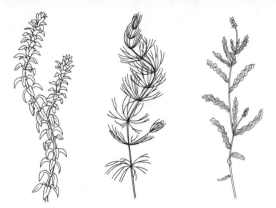

Submergents are plants that grow beneath the water's surface and are attached by roots to the bottom. They characteristically have very thin or finely dissected leaves. This is a useful adaptation because it aids in the exchange of gases between the plant and the water.

Common submergents in ponds and swamps along the Seaway Trail are elodea, water milfoil, hornwort, eelgrass, and curly pondweed. Each year some of the submergent and floating plants die and settle to the bottom. Over a long period of time these deposits, along with sediments washed in by streams and runoff, fill the basin.

Emergents

As organic and mineral sediments are added to the bottom the water depth decreases until eventually plants can become established, rooted on the bottom with stems and leaves protruding from the surface. These are emergents and a variety can be observed in wetlands along the trail. Some of the most common are pickerelweed, cattail, swamp loosestrife, purple loosestrife, arrow arum, and arrowhead.

Shrubs

As the bottom continues to build and water depth decreases, woody plants eventually gain a foothold. Water-loving shrubs or small trees such as pussy willow, speckled alder, red osier dogwood, and buttonbush will begin to grow along the margins and extend inward on areas where the water is shallowest. This stage of swamp development may persist for many years and is probably the stage most often seen along the Seaway Trail.

buttonbush

75

Forest

Along with the shrubs, a few seeds of pioneer tree species will germinate on drier sites. Trees that can survive on very moist soil are red maple, black ash, and, before they were decimated by Dutch elm disease, the American elm. The roots of these trees do not penetrate deeply into the substrate since the water-logged soil has practically no oxygen. Instead they develop shallow root systems and may be uprooted and blown over in high winds. A swamp forest such as this may persist for a very long period of time if regional climatic conditions do not change.

Typical wildlife species of marshes and swamps are ducks, Canada geese, great blue herons, kingfishers, red-wing blackbirds, muskrats, beavers, snapping turtles, and painted turtles. These are described later in this chapter.

great blue heron

Bogs: How They Came to Be

The entire area of the Seaway Trail in Pennsylvania and New York was under a mile high sheet of ice 15,000 years ago. As the glacier retreated large chunks of ice were buried by glacial debris. When these melted, depressions formed and many filled with water, forming lakes and ponds. A fringe of sphagnum moss and other herbaceous plants developed on the moist soil around the margins of some of these bodies of water.

Under conditions ideal for growth, the sphagnum fringe expanded and began to creep out over the water in floating mats. Each year new growth extended the mat farther into the pond and pushed last year's plants deeper into the water. As years passed the floating sphagnum mat steadily closed in on the center of the pond and the basin progressively filled as new growth forming each year forced last year's growth downward. After thousands of years the open water disappeared entirely forming the quaking bog we see today.

The Bog Habitat

The water level is very near the surface in most bogs and walking on one is like walking on a waterbed. Each step causes a wave of motion that is transmitted to the surrounding plants causing them to vibrate. This is the source of the name quaking bog.

The growth of spaghnum moss liberates weak acids which accumulate during development of the bog until it becomes a very acid environment. This and the low oxygen content in the depths of the bog prevent growth of bacteria and fungi of decay. The result is that the bog has great preservative qualities and there is little decomposition of the plant materials that make up the substrate.

Among the plants that thrive under these very special environmental conditions are the insect-trapping plants. These are plants that carry on photosynthesis like other green plants, but also supplement their nutrition by capturing and digesting small insects. This practice may have evolved in response to nitrate and other mineral deficiencies in the bog substrate.

Nitrates are essential for plant growth. They are present in natural soils mainly from the decomposition of plants. In the bog habitat where decomposition is very slow there is a chronic shortage of nitrates and probably other mineral nutrients as well. Pitcher plant and sundew are insectivorous plants commonly present in bogs throughout the northeast.

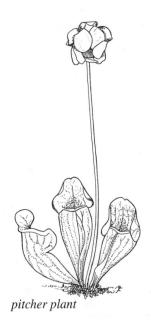

pitcher plant

Several native orchids also prefer the environmental conditions found in bogs. Orchids evolved in the tropics and the greatest number of species grow there today, often on the trunks of trees. With regard to nutrient availability there is some similarity between this habitat and the one occupied by bog orchids. One should visit a bog in late June or early July to enjoy the rare treat of observing the native orchids in flower. The ones most likely to be seen are grass pink, rose pogonia, and mocassin flower.

Low-growing members of the heath

family are the chief plants of the bog shrub community. Although these plants are often growing with their roots in water they have leaf features characteristic of plants that grow in very dry environments. These traits for conserving water include waxy coatings, rolled under margins, and scaly, fuzzy, or woolly undercoatings. It was originally thought that even though they were growing in water, the roots could not absorb the acid bog water. More recent investigations indicate that these water conserving features may be a response to the low nutrient level of the bog substrate rather than the high acidity.

grass pink

All of the bog shrubs of the heath family, except leatherleaf and cranberry, have leaves with the margins rolled under. Leatherleaf has leaves with an undercoating of brown scales; bog rosemary has blue-green leaves with white undersides; Labrador tea has leaves with dense, wooly undersides; bog laurel has dark green, shiny leaves with white undercoatings; and cranberry has very small leaves with white undersides.

From the earliest of times people have considered bogs to be strange and forbidding places. One early writer even referred to them as "trysting places for witches." They are indeed unique habitats and their unfamiliarity has probably been responsible for these reactions of fear and foreboding. A possible contributing factor has been a consequence of their preservative qualities. Like natural mausoleums, bogs have yielded the preserved bodies of long extinct ice age mammals such as mastodons and mammoths. In Europe, where peat is often dug as a fuel, 2000-year-old preserved bodies of humans have been uncovered that seem to have been buried as a ritual or a form of execution.

The preservative nature of bogs has been useful to scientists studying the history of forests in New York State. Over the thousands of years it took for the bog basin to fill, the pollen from local plants became part of the yearly accumulation. The trees in the northeast are 60-80% wind-pollinated and produce an abundance of pollen that is blown about by the wind and some deposited in bogs.

Using a special type of sampling device, biologists have been able to take samples of peat from all levels of the bog. Fortunately, each species of tree produces a different type of pollen and they are all preserved in the peat. By identifying the pollen at a given level the biologist can tell what trees were growing in the vicinity of the bog when the peat at that level formed. Studies of this nature have resulted in detailed knowledge of the forests that have existed in central and western New York since the retreat of the last glacier.

The Life History of a Bog

As with swamps, if natural forces are uninterrupted, bogs will eventually become forests. In the beginning of bog development, as the floating spaghnum mat expands, it supports grasses, sedges, and other herbaceous plants such as the native orchids and insectivorous plants. These make up a bog meadow which constitutes the earliest stage in the life of a bog.

Shrubs usually become established among the herbs or, more often, closer to the shoreward margin of the bog meadow. Over a long period of time as the basin fills, the shrubs will spread inward and cover the entire surface of the bog, building up the surface and shading out the herbaceous plants.

Along with the shrub species several pioneer tree species can be observed. These trees, including larch, black spruce, and sometimes white pine and red maple, will after many years become a bog forest that may persist for hundreds of years.

The bog is a harsh environment for pioneer trees and they grow very slowly. A tree only a few feet tall may be 100 or more years old. Since the water level is near the surface, root systems are shallow and the trees are easily toppled by strong winds. A series of wet years can raise the water level enough to kill most of the trees. Therefore, it is not unusual to see a number of dead trees in most bogs.

As a result of erosion or some other natural or man-made force, drainage patterns may change causing the water level of a bog to drop. If this happens the dried peat may be harvested and sold as peat moss.

When a bog has progressed to the forest stage the surface peat has been oxidized and decomposed to a fine black consistency. In many places along the Seaway Trail in central New York State the trees have been removed and drainage ditches dug in these areas to create muck farms. Muck farming is of great economic importance in this region for the production of such crops as celery, lettuce, and onions.

Western and central New York State probably contains more peat bogs than any other area of comparable size in the United States. Many of these are more than 12 acres in size and are thus protected from exploitation by the New York Wetlands Act of 1975. Not only are they of great value as wetlands, they are fascinating places to visit and study.

Blackbirds & Beavers: The Wildlife of Swamps and Ponds

Wetlands provide habitats for a variety of animals that could not survive in any other environment. The animals described here are not all of those that live there but they are ones that are most likely to be seen by any traveler who spends a few summer hours observing wetlands.

Birds

BELTED KINGFISHER: This bird appears to be top-heavy with a large, unevenly crested head, a long, pointed beak, and very short legs with small feet. It has bluish-gray upper parts with a white spot in front of each eye, a white collar, and a bluish-gray band across its white chest. The female is about the same size as the male but has an additional chestnut brown band across her chest.

belted kingfisher

The belted kingfisher is a solitary bird except during the mating season in May. The male and female usually find a vertical bank of exposed sandy or gravelly soil near water and dig a burrow angling slightly upward and up to 15" deep. This is accomplished by digging with their beaks and scratching out the loose soil with their feet. A chamber at the end of the burrow with a layer of grass and leaves is the nest. The female lays five to 14 eggs and incubates them, with little help from the male, for about 24 days.

When the young are still in the nest, their diet consists mainly of fish regurgitated by the parents. After the young birds leave the nest they learn to fish by retrieving dead fish dropped from the perch by the parents. Ten days after leaving the nest the young are able to fish for themselves and they seek their own fishing grounds. The food of adults is mainly fish but they may also eat frogs, lizards, insects, crayfish, and mice.

Their manner of fishing is sometimes startling to someone who is unfamiliar with their habits. From a perch over a pond or stream the bird will suddenly dive head first into the water with a splash. A few seconds later it will emerge with a small fish in its beak which it turns and swallows head first. If the fish is too large its tail may protrude from the beak until the kingfisher's very rapid digestion allows it to slide down the gullet. Later, the indigestible parts such as bones and scales are regurgitated.

Most of the belted kingfishers in the region of the Seaway Trail migrate southward in winter, some as far as South America.

CANADA GOOSE: The Canada or wild goose may be the best known waterfowl on the North American continent. It is a large bird with a wingspan of up to five and 1/2 feet and a weight of up to 18 pounds. The female is smaller than the male but each has a black head with a white patch under the chin that extends up to the cheeks on each side, a black bill, and black feet. During molting there is a period, usually in July, when they lose all the flight feathers in their wings and are grounded.

Canada geese usually build their nests on the ground near water. The nests are constructed of grass, moss, and small sticks, and lined with down. The female lays five to nine eggs, and incubates them 28-30 days as the male stands guard. The young hatch in June and the male leads them to water, continuing to guard them. By September the young are mature enough to join the migration flights. The young usually do not mate until they are three years old at which time they pair for life.

The food of the Canada goose consists of shoots, roots, and seeds of water plants, eelgrass being a favorite. Since they often dig for food with their bills into the bottom mud, they, like ducks, are often victims of lead poisoning by lead pellets from shotgun shells. They also consume large quantities of berries, grain, and insects such as grasshoppers. They can be seen in corn fields after the harvest feeding on grain that has been left behind.

Some Canada geese in the wild have been known to reach an age of 28 years, although most of them do not live as long. In captivity they have been known to live for 33 years.

Wild geese are the harbingers of spring and the predecessors of winter. Anyone in the vicinity of the Seaway Trail in April and October will witness the great vees of geese flying overhead, uttering their characteristic "onk onk." It is not known why geese fly in vees but scientists have suggested that the vee formation is a way of maintaining visual contact and avoiding collisions.

In early days wild geese were much more abundant than they are today. They provided a great quantity of food and feathers for many featherbeds of early settlers. They are still an important game bird as indicated by the more than 100,000 taken by hunters in New York State in a recent hunting season.

GREAT BLUE HERON: Sometimes called blue crane, the great blue heron is the largest common wading bird in North America. It may reach a length of four feet and have a wingspan of five to six feet. Generally, the great blue heron is bluish gray with a black crown and the sides of the head and throat white. It has long, slender legs and neck with a yellowish bill up to six inches long. It can take flight from a floating position in deep water and flies gracefully with slow, steady strokes of its large wings.

It constructs a large nest of interwoven sticks lined with twigs and leaves. The nests are in colonies of a few to many birds, usually in the tops of tall trees near streams, swamps, or lakes. The female lays three to four eggs and incubates them for about 28 days. The clutch size increases northward with an average of five eggs in southern Canada. The young are fed mainly on fish which are eaten by the parent then regurgitated at the nest. By mid-July the young are ready to fly and fish for themselves.

The diet of the great blue heron consists mostly of fish but it includes a variety of animals such as crayfish, frogs, snakes, and even field mice and chipmunks when they can be caught.

To watch as a heron fishes for dinner is a great pleasure. It is a very cautious bird and will not allow a close approach. In shallow water the great blue takes very slow steps, then freezes, staring intently at a spot in the water. Suddenly its long neck flashes out and down and the unfortunate prey is speared or seized by the long beak. Fish of up to a foot in length captured in this manner may disappear down the throat of the bird after they have been turned to go down head first. There are many areas along the Seaway Trail where the patient observer can watch the great blue heron fish for its breakfast or dinner.

The great blue migrates southward as ice begins to form on swamps and ponds. A few may remain in the area in mild winters but most fly southward and some may travel as far south as Colombia and Venezuela. See illustration on p. 76.

MALLARD: The mallard is the most common and widespread of the ducks. They tame easily and are often domesticated around the world. The male or drake has a green head and neck with a white ring, a ruddy breast, and upturned feathers on its tail. The female is smaller with a brown head and no white ring around the neck. The call of the female is a harsh "quack" while the drake sounds like a loud whisper.

In the wild, mallards prefer to build their nests on the ground near water concealed by cattails, reeds, or other vegetation but they are very adaptable. The female lays six to 13 eggs and incubates them 26-28 days. The ducklings leave the nest usually within 24 hours of hatching and go to the water. By late August the surviving young are ready to join the migration flights.

During the summer molting season the female is unable to fly for 32 days, the male for 34 days. The fall migration extends the range of the North American mallard as far south as Panama. Along the Seaway Trail immigrants from farther north may spend the winter in areas where there is open water.

83

The mallard's diet consists of seeds, aquatic vegetation, and insects including great numbers of mosquito larvae. The mallard may be the most valuable of all wild ducks being easy to harvest and an excellent source of food for humans. It made up the largest proportion of the 260,000 ducks taken in a recent year by hunters in New York State. Unfortunately, for every bird taken by hunters, it is estimated that 1400 pellets are left behind in ponds, lakes, and marshes. A single pellet ingested with food can introduce enough lead into its system to kill a duck. Over the years untold thousands have perished of lead poisoning. In a move too late for these victims, beginning in 1991, the use of lead shot in duck hunting became illegal in NYS.

RED-WINGED BLACKBIRD OR EASTERN REDWING: The red-winged blackbird loves marshes and swamps and the wetlands associated with ponds and lakes. During the mating season the male is black with bright scarlet shoulder patches bordered with white or pale yellow. These show when he spreads his wings but are mostly hidden when his wings are folded. The female is smaller and brownish-black with lighter streaks.

During the breeding season each male stakes out a territory and defends it vigorously against any other trespassing red-wing male. One of the warning signals to intruding males by the defender is to spread his wings and prominently display the red shoulder patches. This is usually enough to send the interloper on his way. Researchers found that when they obscured the red patches with a black dye 60% of those males lost their territory to other intruding red-wings. Thus it appears that the red shoulder patches are badges of authority.

The female accepts the site chosen by the male and builds a nest in reeds, cattails, or shrubs by weaving plant materials into a basket and lining it with fine grasses. She lays three to five eggs and incubates them for 11-12 days. During this time the male defends his brood against predators and it is not uncommon to observe a red-wing chasing a crow or hawk. The young are fed entirely on insects.

They may leave the nest before they can fly and scramble about on reeds and branches. Sometimes they fall into the water and are eaten by snapping turtles, frogs, or fish. But since they can swim at the age of five or six days they usually climb out safely.

During the mating season the main food of the red-winged blackbird is insects, but for the rest of the year the seeds of grasses and other herbaceous plants, sometimes including crop plants, make up its diet. In autumn the males form large flocks that forage for food on the uplands during the day then return to a swamp or marsh to roost. Males and females congregate in great flocks for the southward migration and spend the winter south of the Delaware and Ohio River valleys.

Mammals

BEAVERS: With regard to its influence on history, the beaver is one of North America's most important fur-bearing animals. A large rodent that grows throughout its life, it may weigh 30-60 pounds as an adult. Males, females, and immature animals all have rich, dark brown fur on their backs with slightly paler undersides. They have large, webbed hind feet with double claws on two inner toes of each foot. These modified claws serve as comb-like structures for grooming the fur and applying waterproofing oil from two glands under the tail.

A distinctive feature of the beaver is a large, flat tail covered with soft, black scales. In addition to functioning as a rudder for underwater swimming, the tail is also used as a signaling device. When an intruder is spotted the beaver gives a loud slap on the water warning other members of the colony.

Beavers may be best known for their engineering accomplishments. They create ponds and lakes by using twigs, limbs, small trees, and mud to build dams across flowing water. These vary in size but may reach eight to 11 feet in height and 300 feet in length. The impounded water not only serves the beaver as a home site but also

provides an environment for other wildlife species such as minks, muskrats, waterfowl, and fish.

In the pond created by the dam, the beaver builds a lodge of logs, sticks, and mud. The lodges vary in size but when they are first constructed are usually five to six feet high and 20-30 feet in diameter. Each year an additional coating of sticks and mud are added so the lodge grows with time. It has an inner chamber above the water line with a ventilation hole and an underwater tunnel leading to the outside. Sometimes along fast-flowing streams, instead of constructing a lodge, the beaver may dig into a bank forming a burrow that slopes upward to a chamber above the water line with an underwater entrance.

The mating season is January-February and, after a gestation period of about 107 days, the female gives birth usually to two to four fully-furred kits in May or June. At the age of two to three weeks the young begin eating fresh leaves the female has carried in from the outside and by six to eight weeks of age they are weaned. A typical colony consists of two adults, the yearlings and the current year's kits. Beavers are sexually mature at two years of age and either leave the lodge voluntarily or are forced out by the parents. The average life span is 10-12 years but a few live to the ripe old age of 20.

The food of beavers consists entirely of plants. The inner bark of living trees is the main food for most of the year with the favorite being aspen trees less than six inches in diameter. If these are not available, birch, alder, willow, and black cherry are just as readily eaten. During, fall, winter, and spring, twigs and bark of woody plants make up most of their diet but in summer as much as 90% of their food is herbaceous plants.

During autumn and until ice forms the beaver colony collects a supply of food logs and branches which they anchor to the bottom of the pond near the underwater entrance to their lodge. This food cache may be as much as 10' high and 40' in circumference. In the winter months when ice has closed the surface of the pond, the beaver swims to the food pile, chews off a branch and drags it back to the lodge to eat. Depending on their size they need one and 1/2 to four and 1/2 pounds of bark per day to survive.

Beavers are most active at night, spending most of their day sleeping in their lodges. They may occasionally be seen during the day in summer and especially in autumn when they are busy storing food or making dam and lodge repairs. There are several places along the

Seaway Trail where the patient traveler can observe beaver activity, the best time being late afternoon or dusk.

The quest for the fur of the beaver was an important factor in the exploration of North America. As a result of the value of its fur in European markets, the beaver was practically eliminated from the region that would become New York State by the mid-to-late 1600s, except for colonies in the Adirondacks. By 1902 even the Adirondack colonies were gone. In 1903 a few pairs were released in the Adirondack Mountains and, with complete protection by law, they prospered. Today the beaver is the state mammal of New York State with enough abundance to support an annual trapping season. In a recent hunting season, trappers took about 14,000 beaver pelts with a value of less than 10 dollars per pelt.

MUSKRATS: The muskrat resembles the beaver somewhat but is much smaller. Its fur is dark brown on the back, brownish on the sides, and pale gray on the underside. Color variations that are sometimes exhibited are

black, albino, and tan. It has small front feet and large, partially webbed hind feet for efficient swimming. The long, nearly hairless, vertically-compressed tail is blackish-brown and serves as a rudder. The muskrat has small, black, beady eyes, and ears so small they are almost hidden by fur. The male and female are very similar in appearance but the female is slightly smaller. The muskrat is well adapted for a semi-aquatic life and can remain under water for 15 minutes or more.

Depending on environmental conditions muskrats build two kinds of living quarters. In areas where there is little emergent vegetation, a burrow with an underwater entrance is dug into a stream bank or dam. These burrows slope upward to a chamber above the water level lined with grass and shredded herbaceous material. Earthen dams may be seriously damaged and weakened by these burrows if the muskrat population is high.

In wetlands where there is an abundance of cattails and other emergents the muskrat builds a lodge similar to a beaver lodge except it is smaller and usually does not include woody sticks and branches in its construction.

The lodge is located in a marsh or swamp where the water depth is no more than two feet. It is usually three to four feet high and eight to 10' in diameter at the underwater base. Constructed of mud and vegetation the lodge has one or more underwater entrance tunnels and a living chamber lined with plant material. The walls of the chamber are about one foot thick which is sufficient to protect the inhabitants from predators and from the weather. Although they are solitary animals, except during the breeding season, several muskrats may huddle together in a lodge for warmth in winter.

The food of the muskrat is mainly vegetation including the roots, shoots, and young leaves of cattails, arrowhead, bur reed, pickerelweed, and other aquatic plants. Unlike the beaver, animal life may also be a part of the muskrat's diet. It will eat insects, crayfish, frogs, and fish when it can catch them. Freshwater mussels make up an important part of its winter food when it can find them. In its search for food the muskrat must constantly be on guard against predators whose food it would become. These include snapping turtles, foxes, weasels, great horned owls, minks, and raccoons.

The breeding season for muskrats may extend from March to October. After a gestation period of 25-30 days the female gives birth to six or seven young. The kits grow rapidly and are able to swim before they open their eyes in about two weeks. They are weaned in about four weeks and soon leave the home lodge for territories of their own. The female may produce two or three litters in a breeding season. The average life span of a muskrat in the wild is three to four years.

Because of its abundance and availability the muskrat may be the most valuable of all fur-bearing animals in North America today. It is marketed under the trade names Hudson seal, Russian otter, red seal, and river mink. Over 200,000 muskrat pelts per year are harvested in Pennsylvania and in a recent trapping season more than 122,000 were harvested by New York State trappers.

Reptiles

PAINTED TURTLES: The largest painted turtles may have an upper shell seven inches long and four inches wide but the average size is smaller. The shell is olive to black with red markings around the edge. The

painted turtle

head has yellow stripes and there is a yellow line behind each eye. The lower shell of the painted turtle is yellow with a darkened central figure that extends from front to back.

Sexual maturity seems related to size rather than age with the male maturing when the lower shell is 3 and 1/2 inches long. This usually occurs during spring of the fifth year. The female matures sexually when the lower shell is about four inches in length which takes place in spring of the sixth year. Mating occurs from March to June and the female begins laying eggs in late May. In an open space she digs a nest about four inches deep with her hind feet, deposits three to 10 eggs, covers them with the excavated soil and returns to the pond. These hatch in about 76 days in mid-to-late August and the young dig themselves out and head for water. If the eggs are laid at a later date the young may spend the winter in the nest or the eggs may not hatch until the following spring.

The food of painted turtles consists of both plant and animal matter. Almost any aquatic organisms small enough to swallow may become part of the turtle's dinner. A captured animal too large to swallow may be held in the jaws and torn apart with the front claws. Almost all the food of growing young painted turtles is small aquatic animals but as they grow older they eat more plant food. Among the plants eaten are algae, cattail seeds and young stems, and duckweed.

The painted turtle is probably the most abundant turtle in the swamps and ponds along the Seaway Trail. On almost any sunny day in summer they can be seen in groups sunning themselves on logs and rocks. This time out of water reduces the algal growth on their shells and the number of leeches and other aquatic skin parasites. They are active during the day and spend the night sleeping on the bottom or on partially submerged logs or rocks. In winter when ice covers the water the painted turtle hibernates by burrowing as much as 12" into bottom mud.

SNAPPING TURTLE: The snapping turtle may be the largest of the freshwater turtles with adults weighing up to 30 pounds and having a shell 18-19" in diameter. One raised in captivity is reported to have weighed 86 pounds. The shell is made up of three rows of brownish-black plates and has a saw-toothed rear margin. The cross-shaped lower shell is yellowish and does not cover the legs, neck, and tail. The snapping turtle has a large head and powerful jaws, the upper one somewhat hooked. It has a vicious temper and when out of water will aggressively attack anyone or anything if it is annoyed. When they close their jaws on an object, they hang on, resulting in the superstition that they will not let go until sundown. They continue to grow throughout their lives but the rate of growth seems to decline with age. Snapping turtles have a life span that may exceed 25 years.

Sexual maturity is reached when the shell is about eight inches long and mating occurs from April to November. The peak egg laying time is June. The female leaves the water and finds an open site that may be as much as 100 yards or more from the water. She digs a cavity four to seven inches deep with her hind feet and deposits 20-40 eggs. When egg laying is complete she covers the eggs with soil and returns to the water. More than half of these nests are usually destroyed by skunks, raccoons, and minks for whom the eggs are a tasty treat.

The eggs in the unmolested nests undergo a long period of incubation and the young emerge in late August to early October. In some instances they do not emerge until the following spring.

When the eggs hatch the young dig their way out of the nest and head for the water. At this age they may become the prey of herons, crows, hawks, frogs, fish, and snakes. While mature snapping turtles have no natural enemies, their biggest threat may be toxic substances in the environment and destruction of habitat by human activities.

These turtles may occur in many of the types of wetlands. They prefer bodies of water with lots of submerged logs and brush, soft mud bottoms, and an abundance of aquatic vegetation. Unlike many other turtles, they have high water loss at elevated temperatures so they do not crawl out on rocks or logs to bask in the sun. They may float just below the water surface, however, with only eyes and nostrils protruding.

snapping turtle

90

Although appearing sluggish during the day, the snapping turtle is very active searching for food at night and it can remain underwater for 15 minutes or more. Its food is mostly animal matter and includes almost anything that moves within its reach. It is also known to dine on aquatic plants. In October it burrows into the bottom mud, often with other turtles, where it hibernates until April.

The flesh of the snapping turtle is very edible and is especially delicious in soups and stews. In former times these turtles were sometimes fattened for food in farm swill barrels. The eggs are edible if fried but they will not hard boil. This turtle is no longer extensively taken for food. Although it may take some of the duckling population, it is valuable for the ecosystem as a scavenger and predator.

Cranberry & Cattails: The Plants of Swamps and Bogs

The plants described here are ones that are common in the wetlands along the Seaway Trail in Pennsylvania and New York. One or more of these is almost certain to be seen in any wetland the interested traveler may wish to stop and observe. Descriptions are brief but with the drawings should be complete enough for identification of the plants.

Bog Plants

GRASS PINK: Flowering time: June-July; flowers: 2" wide, pink to deep rose with a crest of yellow hairs, at tip of stem about 1' high; one leaf long and grass-like, attached to base of stem. This is a native orchid and all native orchids are protected by New York State law. See illustration on p. 78.

LARGE CRANBERRY: Flowering time: June-August; flowers: pink, on long stalks from the middle of stem, hanging downward, petals 4, bent backward, stamens protruding as a yellow cone in the center of the flower; leaves: small, about 3/4 of an inch long, with white undersides, evergreen; stems trailing over the surface of the bog with upright branches. This is the commercial cranberry which is cultivated on Cape Cod. They are sometimes harvested for local use by individuals who live near bogs.

MOCCASIN FLOWER: Flowering time: May-June; flowers: pink with deeply colored veins, 1 large flower at the tip of a leafless stem about 1' high; leaves: two prominently veined, arising from base of stem. This is a native orchid and protected by law.

PITCHER PLANT: Flowering time: May-June; flowers: a single, large flower, nodding, with 5 dark red petals on a long stalk, petals fall in a few days but the stalk with the seed pod may persist into the next growing season; leaves: at the base of the flower stalk are hollow and pitcher-shaped with a bristly upper extension and a wing down one side. The 6-8" long pitcher-like leaves usually contain water and serve as insect traps. The trapped insects are digested by digestive juices in the water. The Pitcher Plant is protected by law and should not be collected. See illustration p. 77.

ROSE POGONIA: Flowering time: June-July; flowers: rose-pink, central lip of flower covered with yellow hairs, single flower at tip of stem about 1' high; leaves: one small leaf slightly below the flower and another larger one, about 4" long, attached about the midpoint on the stem. This is a native orchid protected by law.

ROUND-LEAVED SUNDEW: Flowering time: June-August; flowers: small, white, in a cluster at the tip of a leafless stalk that is usually 4-6" high; leaves: in a basal rosette, circular in outline and on long stalks, covered with hairs, each hair with a drop of sticky substance at its tip. When a tiny insect lands on the leaf it becomes trapped in the sticky substance and over a period of hours the leaf closes over it like closing the hand over an object in the palm. When the insect is digested the leaf reopens and the trap is reset. Sundews are protected by New York State law.

SPATULA-SHAPED SUNDEW: Very similar to round-leaved sundew but the leaves are oval-shaped with the widest part above the middle. In some bogs this species is more common than round-leaved sundew.

Pond and Swamp Plants

ARROW ARUM: Flowering time: May-June; flowers: small and inconspicuous, enclosed in a green, tubular, pointed structure with a slit along one side called a spathe, on a long stalk, at maturity the flower stalk bends until the spathe is under water or near the ground; leaves: broadly arrow-shaped with 3 prominent nerves and long stalks. This is a very common emergent and is found in most of the swamps and pond margins along the Seaway Trail. See illustration on p. 74.

BROAD-LEAVED ARROWHEAD: Flowering time: July-September; flowers: white with 3 petals, in clusters at tip of a leafless stem 1-2' high, male flowers with short stalks at top of stem, female flowers with longer stalks beneath them; leaves: arrow-shaped on stalks usually as long as the water is deep so leaves are always above the water. They produce tubers eaten by ducks, geese, and muskrats, and were used for food by American Indians. See illustration on p. 74.

BROAD-LEAVED CATTAIL: Flowering time: May-July; flowers: tiny, inconspicuous, crowded in cylindrical clusters, or cattails, at the tips of long stalks that may be 4-8' high, the flower cluster, with male flowers at the top and female flowers beneath, is about 1" in diameter. Dried cattail leaves are used in making braided rush bottom chairs. See illustration on p. 74.

NARROW-LEAVED CATTAIL OR NAILROD: Very similar to broad-leaved cattail but the leaves are only 1/2" wide and the flower cluster is only 1/2" in diameter. The male flowers at the top are separated by a few centimeters from the lower female flowers. See illustration on p. 74.

GIANT BUR-REED: Flowering time: July-September: flowers: in whitish or greenish balls at the top of the stem which is usually 1-2' high, the lower clusters are female flowers that become bur-like seed pods; leaves: long, grass-like, in two rows, each with a ridge on the underside.

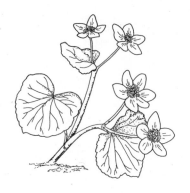

MARSH MARIGOLD: Flowering time: April-May; flowers: bright yellow with 5-9 petal-like parts; leaves: shiny green, heart-shaped at the base but with rounded tips, on long stalks; stems hollow. These plants often occur in masses and are spectacular when in flower.

PICKERELWEED: Flowering time: July-September; flowers: blue, densely clustered at the top of the stem, each has 3 upper and 3 lower lobes with a yellow spot on the middle upper lobe; leaves: small, sheath-like leaf at the base of the flower cluster, a single larger leaf attached to the base of the stem, large leaf heart-shaped at the base and tapering to a blunt point. This is an emergent usually with the leaves and the flower cluster above the water. See illustration on p. 74.

PURPLE LOOSESTRIFE: Flowering time: July-September; flowers: pink to red-purple, in long clusters at the tips of stems and branches, petals 5 or 6, some flowers produce both green and yellow pollen; leaves: in pairs or in 3's; stems may get 4-5' high. This is a plant pest introduced from Europe that is spreading rapidly in wetlands. Also illustrated on p. 74.

SWAMP LOOSESTRIFE: Flowering time: May-October; flowers: pink to rose, in clusters in the axils of upper leaves, 5 petals tapering at their base; leaves: mostly in 3's or 4's; stems bending, often touching the ground or water at the tip, forming new roots at that point, usually 3-4' long. Unlike purple loosestrife, this is a native species and a valuable part of the ecosystem. See illustration on p. 74.

SPATTERDOCK: Flowering time: May-October; flowers: yellow, 3" wide, on long stalks, floating on the surface of the water; leaves: floating up to 1' long with rounded tips and heart-shaped bases often with overlapping lobes, with long stalks that are attached to the bottom. The seeds of this plant are an important food for waterfowl and the leaves are eaten by beavers and other aquatic animals.

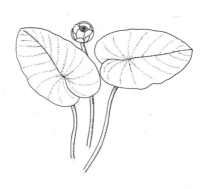

WHITE WATER LILY OR FRAGRANT WATER LILY: Flowering time: June-September; flowers: white, up to 6" wide, very fragrant, floating on long stalks; opening in the morning and closing in the afternoon; leaves: floating, almost round, up to 10" wide, purplish on the underside, on stalks that extend to the bottom of the pond. The seeds and other parts are eaten by marsh birds, waterfowl, muskrats, beavers, moose, and deer.

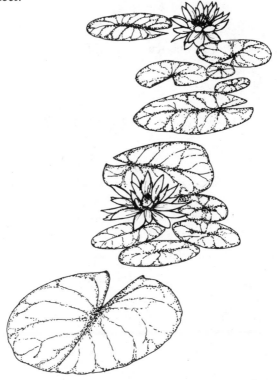

Chapter V

SAND DUNES & SANDY BEACHES

"Sand is a substance that is beautiful, mysterious, and infinitely variable; each grain on a beach is the result of processes that go back into the shadowy beginnings of life, or of the earth itself"
- Rachel Carson

Origin of the Great Lakes

The Seaway Trail follows the shoreline of two of the lakes - Erie and Ontario - that are part of the greatest reservoir of fresh water on earth.

The Great Lakes owe their origin to the advance and retreat of glaciers over North America. In the last million years four ice sheets have moved southward then melted back. As these glaciers advanced they took the paths of least resistance like streams of flowing water. They covered New England, New York, and parts of Pennsylvania, but the Appalachian Mountains slowed their progress in the east.

In the midwestern states the ice moved much farther south. As they moved southward, the glaciers gouged and scoured the surface of the land. In places where there were softer rock layers the gouging was deeper and some of the depressions that formed became the basins for the Finger Lakes and the Great Lakes. The same type of gouging left columns of harder rock in the upper St. Lawrence Valley that today we call the Thousand Islands.

The last ice sheet advanced about 50,000 years ago and melted from New York State about 10,000 years ago. In many areas along the Seaway Trail where rock layers are exposed, polished rock surfaces and scratches are testimony to the last glacier's passage and its direction of movement.

illustration by Ruth Sachidanandan

About Lake Erie and Lake Ontario

Lake Erie and Lake Ontario are the smallest of the Great Lakes. The Great Lakes system contains 95% of the surface fresh water in the United States and 20% of the surface fresh water in the world.

Lake Erie ranks as #12 in the world in surface area, but is the shallowest and contains the least volume of water of any of the Great Lakes. At its deepest point, about 30 miles northeast of Erie, Pennsylvania, Lake Erie is about 210' deep, but its average depth is only 58'. The shallowest part is the western end where the depth is between 25 and 35'.

Lake Ontario is ranked #14 in the world in surface area but is the smallest of the Great Lakes. It is the third deepest, after Lake Superior and Lake Michigan. The deepest point in Lake Ontario is about 18 miles northeast of Sodus Point, New York, where the depth is 778'. It receives the drainage from all the other lakes through the Niagara River which carries 80% of all its inflowing water. Draining into the North Atlantic through the St. Lawrence River, the amount of water that flows out of Lake Ontario in 10 minutes is enough to supply the needs of New York City for a day.

Unfortunately, all of the Great Lakes are polluted but Lake Erie and Lake Ontario are the first and second-most polluted respectively. Contributing factors to the pollution of Lake Erie are its shallow depths and the many industrial and population centers along its margins in both Canada and the United States. Lake Ontario receives polluted water directly from Lake Erie in addition to its own pollution from human activities. Although some of the pollutants in these lakes are toxic to humans they are present in such low concentrations that the lakes serve as sources of municipal water for many communities along their shores.

Through aquatic food chains some toxic pollutants may become so concentrated in fish that they are unsafe for human consumption. When a fishing license is issued in New York State it is accompanied by suggestions about the species and quantity of fish that can safely be eaten from Lake Ontario and other waters in the state.

The Origin of Sands and Beaches

The Great Lakes are like inland freshwater oceans in many ways, but in one important way they are not - they do not have ocean tides. Otherwise they behave like great bodies of water and have their own history and folklore of outstanding events and heroic deeds. These events are well-chronicled in several fine museums along the Trail.

Storms on the lakes can produce waves similar to those observed on many seacoasts. Steep weather-beaten cliffs, broad sand or cobble beaches, and the exposed faces of glacial deposits, such as those at Chimney Bluffs in Wayne County, New York, all provide abundant evidence of wave action not unlike seashores. The interested traveler can observe all of these features along the Seaway Trail on the shores of Lakes Erie and Ontario.

Perhaps of more general interest are the sand and cobble beaches along the trail. Cobble beaches are common along the southern shores of Lake Ontario. They consist of rocks of various sizes, from gravels to boulders, which are smooth and rounded from thousands of years of water and ice abrasion. The source of the cobbles is the glacial deposits that were eroded by wave action in the formation of the beach.

The cobble beaches were a prime source for raw materials in the construction of cobblestone houses commonly observed in Niagara and Orleans Counties.

The sand beaches are the primary subject for the remainder of this chapter because of their biological significance and their recreational potential.

Lake Erie and Lake Ontario are oriented with their long axes roughly in an east-west direction and they drain to the east. Consequently, the movement of surface water in these lakes is in an easterly direction. All of the Great Lakes are in the prevailing westerlies wind belt in which winds generally blow from the southwest to the northeast. As a result, in Lakes Erie and Ontario both the surface flow and wind-generated waves move toward the east. Consequently, there is a system of barrier beaches and sand dunes on the eastern shore of Lake Ontario. The dunes here are the largest and most extensive freshwater dunes in New York State. These dunes, which are 70' high in some areas, are the highest in the northeast outside of Cape Cod.

A Dune is Born

When the wind blows across a sandy expanse it picks up grains of sand and bounces them along the surface dislodging other grains which bounce along dislodging still others. Any object in the path of the wind will reduce its speed and sand will be dropped around the object. It may be a rock, a log, a single plant or a clump of plants. A small pile of sand is formed and an embryonic dune is born. As this small mound slowly grows it merges with other mounds which merge with still others until eventually a hillock is formed with a ridge having a gently sloping windward side and a very steep leeward side.

Under a steady wind with nothing to anchor the sand, the dune will continue to grow and to move with the wind. The movement is usually only a few feet per year as the sand grains are rolled up the gentle windward slope and tumble down the steep backside. The movement of the dune is relentless and if the sand is not stabilized it will bury everything in its path.

Usually, in undisturbed coastal environments, dunes are stabilized by the natural growth of plants. One plant in particular, beach grass, is of great importance in this process. When beach grass has become established on it, the dune can continue to grow if there is a source of sand. The beach grass reduces the velocity of the wind so that the sand grains are deposited and they no longer roll over the leeward side. The dune is stabilized and no longer moves with the wind.

The largest sand dunes along the Seaway Trail are located in a stretch of shoreline on the eastern margin of Lake Ontario bordered on the south by the mouth of the Salmon River and on the north by Stony Point along New York Route 3. Some of these dunes are very close to the water's edge and are currently being eroded by wave action.

In order for such dunes to have formed there must have been a fairly extensive source of sand, much more extensive than is provided by the present beaches in this area. It has been estimated that the water level of the lake must have been some 30' lower than it is today in order to expose enough beach sand for building the present dunes. This is believed to have occurred about 5,000 years ago when the northeast was in its driest period since the retreat of the glacier. At that time the current dunes were probably about one mile from the edge of the water.

Wind and Waves

Along a shoreline where dunes are developing there is always a rather extensive beach. The lower beach usually does not have plants growing on it because it is periodically eroded and reformed by waves. Above the wave line sand can begin to accumulate into foredunes. These will move inland with the wind until a plant cover has developed that will bind the sand and anchor the dune. By the time this happens other foredunes have formed on the windward side and a system of foredunes and backdunes has become established.

When only the Indians of the Iroquois Confederacy walked the eastern shore of Lake Ontario the high dunes were covered by forests of beech, birch, oak, hemlock, maple, and other climax forest species. These dunes are remnants of a former time thousands of years ago when the lakeshore was a mile to the west and the intervening distance was a sandy expanse of foredunes and backdunes.

Since then the lake level has risen and the foredunes have eroded leaving very little of that extensive dune

beach grass

system. Some of the dunes that supported forest vegetation for more than a thousand years are now being worn away by waves. Wave action is usually greatest during spring storms after the ice has melted and the water level is at a peak. Erosion may also be severe during high winds that push the water to the eastern end of the lake raising the water level to higher than normal levels.

The State of New York has acquired several tracts of land along the eastern shore of Lake Ontario in an effort to preserve the unique dune environments and the wetlands behind them. Some of these have been developed for recreation and are operated during the summer as public swimming beaches. Other tracts, such as Deer Creek Marsh and Black Pond Wildlife Management Areas, were purchased for reclamation and preservation and are open to the public only to a limited degree. One tract adjacent to state land, the El Dorado Beach Preserve, has been acquired and is managed by The Nature Conservancy. The Preserve is open to the public for nature hikes only. The Sandy Pond Beach Preserve is jointly managed by The Nature Conservancy and the NYS Department of Environmental Conservation to provide public access for day use and to protect the dunes.

Reclamation activities have included putting up snow fences to halt sand erosion and initiate dune building along with the planting of beach grass to stabilize existing dunes. Human activities such as pedestrian traffic and off-the-road vehicles have caused the greatest problems for conservation workers.

Foredunes stabilized by beach grass are very fragile ecosystems that are easily disturbed. A trail made by human or vehicle traffic across the dune may destroy some of the plants and cause a slight notch in its profile. Even on an undisturbed dune, the wind moving over it has a greater speed at the top than at beach level. A notch in the top of the dune funnels the wind and may double its velocity. This increases its erosive force and the result may be a blowout that starts the sand moving and the once-stabilized dune is on the move again.

Life in the Sand

A sand dune provides a harsh environment for plant growth. One of the reasons is that sand is very poor in mineral nutrients. Most of the nutrients that plants must have to grow are held on the surfaces of

beach pea

microscopic soil particles called micelles. These are most common in fine textured soils that contain clay, silt, and decomposed organic matter. Sand has a very coarse texture with little decomposing organic matter and few mineral-holding micelles. Spray from waves during heavy storms and rainfall are the main sources of mineral nutrients for plants growing on the dunes of Lake Ontario.

Another problem experienced by plants growing on dunes is obtaining moisture. The water that is used by plants is held as a film around the soil particles. The maximum thickness of this film is about the same regardless of the size of the particle. The coarse textured sand cannot hold as much water as soils made up of more numerous, smaller particles.

To make matters worse, on sunny days in summer the temperature of the sand may get to 115°F or higher, completely drying out the surface layers. It is not surprising, therefore, that plants which can survive on sand dunes such as beach grass, sea rocket, seaside spurge, and beach pea have root systems that penetrate to a depth below the hot, dry surface sand. The main source of water for these plants is rainfall that percolates downward to the root level. During long dry spells the condensation of dew on sand grains below the surface of the dune may contribute to the survival of dune species.

Constantly shifting sand presents another challenge to the survival of dune plants. If all other factors were favorable, periodic burial by sand would be enough to keep most plants from growing there. Being buried by sand actually stimulates beach grass to more vigorous growth. This plant has a horizontal stem under the sand that sends up branches as it grows. On the surface these sometimes look like planted rows of plants. As the wind blows over the dune and sand builds up around the plant its stem grows longer, always keeping the leaves above the sand. If the leaves are buried, buds in the leaf axils begin to grow and emerge from the sand as new shoots. The continuing growth of stems and leaves is accompanied by formation of an extensive root system that binds the sand together, anchoring the dune.

These characteristics make beach grass very well qualified to survive in sand dune environments. It is without doubt the best dune anchoring plant along the Great Lakes and Atlantic coastlines. Its scientific name, *Ammophilia*, appropriately means "lover of sand."

Life History of a Dune

Like bogs, swamps, and abandoned fields, sand dunes, if left to natural forces, will eventually be claimed by the forest. It begins when a dune is anchored by beach grass and stops moving. This may happen when the dune is fairly small but if there is a source of sand it may continue to grow as did some of the ancient established dunes along the eastern shore of Lake Ontario.

Both of these stages, the dune anchored by beach grass and the forest-covered dune, can be observed along the eastern shore but in origin they are separated by the passage of a vast period of time. It has been estimated that a thousand years may be required for a dune to reach the climax forest stage.

Beach grass is the primary dune building plant but there are others that can survive the rigors of the sand environment. One of these is sea rocket, a member of the mustard family that grows on the upper beach or the lower windward side of the foredunes. It is an annual that completes its life cycle from seed to seed during the summer growing season. Thick leaves that store water and a deeply penetrating root system contribute to its survival in the sand.

Other plants that are able to grow on the sand of the upper beach or foredune are seaside spurge, wormwood, and beach pea. Like sea rocket, seaside spurge completes its life cycle in one summer of growth. It spends the winter as a seed buried in sand by the shifting winds of autumn and germinates in the showers and sunshine of May. Seaside spurge is a tiny ground-hugging plant that may be overlooked unless one is specifically looking for it. Survival in the high summer temperatures is possible because it has a root system that penetrates to the moist layers below the hot, dry surface layer of sand.

Wormwood requires two years to complete its life cycle. During the first year of growth it forms a bushy rosette of leaves on the surface of the sand and a deep taproot. It winters as a taproot containing a reserve of stored food buried in the sand. In the summer of the second season, a tall, leafy stem produces flowers and many wind-scattered seeds, then the plant dies. Wormwood and a closely related

sea rocket

introduced species, dusty miller, are common on beaches and dunes along the Atlantic coast.

Like beach grass, the beach pea has a stem that grows horizontally under the sand sending up new green sprouts each spring. It brightens the dunes with masses of colorful flowers throughout summer. Beach pea is in the same family of plants as the cultivated pea, and, according to some natural food advocates, the very young tender seeds taste like garden peas. An important feature of beach pea is that it has nitrogen-fixing nodules on its roots so that in addition to helping stabilize the sand it also adds enrichment.

These five species - beach grass, sea rocket, seaside spurge, wormwood, and beach pea - are all important dune stabilizers that can be seen on the beaches and foredunes along the eastern shore of Lake Ontario. Over a very long period of time as these plants grow, die, and are buried by sand, small amounts of organic matter accumulate. The result is a slight increase in the water holding ability and nutrient level of the sand. Other plants that could not have survived before may now be able to grow on the dunes or in the swales behind them. Among these are herbaceous plants such as nodding wild rye, starflowered Solomon's seal, evening primrose, and silverweed. These plants are often accompanied by shrubs such as sand cherry, sand dune willow, and other shrubby sand-loving willows.

Most trees are killed if their trunks are buried by sand but this is not so of cottonwoods. If sand builds up around the trunk of a cottonwood it responds by sprouting new roots at a higher level on the trunk. The more deeply buried roots may die for lack of oxygen but the new roots enable the tree to grow and keep pace with accumulating sand. A later blowout that uncovers the trunk may reveal several sets of branch roots, each marking the root level of a previous burial. Commonly associated with the shrub and cottonwood stage of dune succession are sprawling or climbing plants such as poison ivy, wild grape, and greenbriar.

grapevine

Dunes with a few cottonwood trees and dunes covered with forest can be seen along the Seaway Trail on Lake Ontario's eastern shore. The changes that took place in getting from the first to the second stage are mostly unknown since there are very few in-between dunes to observe. From studies of the dunes in other places it is known to have taken a very long time. A major concern today is protection of these fragile ecosystems from destruction by human activities. This has been the aim of New York State agencies and The Nature Conservancy in purchasing large tracts along the eastern shore.

Travelers along the Seaway Trail have access to sandy beaches and dunes at several places. Some of these are privately owned but most are managed by agencies of New York State. These are wonderful recreational areas that with intelligent use can be maintained indefinitely as a service to the public.

The recommended practice is to restrict recreational activities such as picnicking and sunbathing to the beach areas. Use of the dunes for these activities runs the risk of initiating blowouts with the destruction or major damage to dune ecosystems. Away from the beach area it is recommended that visitors stay on approved trails which include protective dune walkover bridges. By following these practices the dune ecosystems can be enjoyed again and again without destroying their natural beauty.

Dune Dwellers

There is animal life in the sand of beaches and dunes but it consists mainly of small creatures such as insects and spiders. Among the larger animals the most commonly seen are birds that have life cycles closely associated with Lake Ontario. Some of these feed on fish or small aquatic animals with the lake as their main source and some make use of beaches and dunes for nesting sites. Unlike the pond, open field, and forest, there are no mammals along the lake that are characterized as dune animals. However, predators such as foxes and weasels may stalk the beaches and dunes for birds, eggs, and young.

Two common birds that can be observed along the beaches of the Seaway Trail are the herring gull and the ring-billed gull. These are very similar but the ring-billed gull is slightly smaller. They both have black wing tips and gray backs with white heads and under parts. When seen together on a sand bar or beach the difference in

ring-billed gull   herring gull

size is noticeable. When observed at closer range the herring gull can be recognized by flesh-colored legs. The ring-billed gull has greenish-yellow feet and legs and a black ring around its beak.

At one time the eastern shore of Lake Ontario was the fishing grounds for the bald eagle and the beaches were the nesting sites for the piping plover. Both of these species are very sensitive to human activities and today they are rare and endangered. The El Dorado Beach Preserve, located at the northern end of the eastern Lake Ontario sand dune region, contains a relatively undisturbed dune ecosystem.

The last breeding eagles were observed in this area in the 1950's but The Nature Conservancy believes that if an undisturbed environment can be maintained both bald eagles and piping plovers may return. Migrant and immature eagles are regular visitors passing through the area. Swimming and picnicking are not permitted on this preserve but it can be visited by birdwatchers and naturalists.

The eastern shore is a refueling stop for many migratory shorebirds. These birds use the beaches to rest and feed before they resume their sometimes very long migratory flights. A plant that is important in this feeding is a green alga called cladophora. In the water it may appear to be a green slimy mass but as seen under the microscope it is made up of slender green filaments. Normally these grow in great numbers attached to the bottom where they are a source of food for many small crustaceans and aquatic insects. During storms or unusually high waves great quantities of filaments may be torn free and washed ashore taking many small organisms with them. These masses of cladophora with their cargoes of aquatic animals are important sources of food for the migrating shorebirds.

Primrose & Wormwood: The Plants of Dunes and Beaches

The following brief descriptions are of plants typically growing on the upper beach and foredunes along the shores of Lake Erie and Lake Ontario. Descriptions and drawings should make it possible to identify the plants. When visiting, please respect these fragile environments and use protective walkovers and trails.

BEACH GRASS: Flowering time: July-September; flowers: small, greenish, inconspicuous, in a crowded cluster at the top a long talk 1-2' high; leaves: several, narrow, arising as a cluster from base of the plant, 2-3' long, flat at their base, with edges rolled under toward tip. See illustration on p. 100.

BEACH PEA: Flowering time: June-August; flowers: purple, in clusters of 5-10 on long stalks from the axils of leaves, later becoming clusters of pea-like pods; leaves: alternate, compound, with 2-12 leaflets and a tendril at the tip; stems creeping over the sand with upturned ends. See illustration on p. 102.

EVENING PRIMROSE: Flowering time: June-October; flowers: yellow, numerous, often crowded at the ends of stems and branches, stigma cross-shaped, 4 petals and 4 turned-back sepals; leaves: lance-shaped, often with wavy margins; stems often reddish, usually 3-4' high.

NODDING WILD RYE: Flowering time: July-October; flowers: greenish, crowded together at the tip of the stem, the whole cluster bent slightly downward; leaves: 4-9, grass-like, up to 3/4" wide; stem 2-5' high.

SEA ROCKET: Flowering time: June-September; flowers: white to pale purple, about 1/3" wide, 4 petals, 4 sepals; leaves: alternate, with wavy-toothed or lobed margins; stems up to 16" high, usually bushy branched. See illustration on p. 104.

SEASIDE SPURGE: Flowering time: July-October; flowers: small and inconspicuous without petals and sepals; leaves: in pairs, pale green, about 3/5" long; stems red, freely branched, lying on the sand; plants with milky juice.

SILVERWEED: Flowering time: June-August; flowers: yellow, about 1" wide, with 5 petals, on leafless stalks; leaves: alternate, compound with 7-25 toothed leaflets, larger ones near the tip of the leaf, all with silvery, silky hairs on the underside; plants with long creeping runners which root at intervals and produce new clusters of leaves.

STAR-FLOWERED SOLOMON'S SEAL: Flowering time: May-August; flowers: small, white, in a long cluster at the tip of the stem, the flower cluster becoming a cluster of berries at first green, then turning almost black or with black strips; leaves: 7-12, alternate, 3-6" long; stems zigzagging between leaves, usually 1-2' tall.

WORMWOOD: Flowering time: July-October; flowers: heads green, nodding, crowded in a branched cluster at the tip of the stem; leaves: finely dissected; stems very leafy, unbranched, usually 2-3' high.

Chapter VI

A TRAVELERS GUIDE TO THE NATURAL HISTORY OF THE SEAWAY TRAIL

This chapter presents travelers with 127 sites of natural history interest found along or near New York State's Lake Erie, Niagara River, Lake Ontario, and St. Lawrence River shoreline. Nature centers, wildlife refuges, state parks, zoos, and trails in each of the Seaway Trail's 11 counties are divided into three segments.

The western segment includes Seaway Trail Pennsylvania which begins at the Ohio state line and follows Pennsylvania Route 5 through Erie County, Pennsylvania to the New York State border. NYS' Seaway Trail then passes through Chautauqua, Erie and Niagara Counties, New York.

In the central segment the trail passes through Orleans, Monroe, Wayne and Cayuga Counties, New York.

The northeastern segment extends from Oswego County through Jefferson and St. Lawrence Counties to the Seaway International Bridge to Canada at Rooseveltown.

Located and described in each of these segments are state and national parks and preserves, public beaches, natural areas, and other points of interest to regional natural history.

Based on information current at the time of writing, the facilities described below are open to the public. Most are within 10 miles, or less, of the Seaway Trail. A few outstanding facilities to which the trail offers access are more than 10 miles from the trail; distances are included in the descriptions. Where there was a charge for admission at the time of writing, this is noted. Most of the state parks have a vehicle fee for day use and a charge for campsites. These have not been noted.

The information for each entry was compiled by making personal visits and observations and by perusing brochures and public information releases.

Most of the areas listed in the following pages are owned and managed by municipal, county, or state governments. In order to preserve these facilities for the next visitor and the next generation, it is necessary to comply with the rules and regulations regarding their use.

Plants and animals growing wild is what natural areas are all about. They should not be molested in any way. Wildflowers are most beautiful when growing in their natural settings. Nothing mars a beautiful area more than the sight of an empty beer can, a discarded candy wrapper, or someone's garbage. Natural areas can be kept looking natural by the proper disposal of trash.

It is suggested that travelers call ahead to verify current operating hours and any admission/use charges.

SEAWAY TRAIL PENNSYLVANIA:
ERIE COUNTY, PA

1. PRESQUE ISLE STATE PARK
Peninsula Drive, Erie, PA; 814-871-4251

Presque Isle State Park is a 3200-acre sandy peninsula jutting seven miles into Lake Erie at Erie, Pennsylvania. The park includes 18 sandy swimming beaches, nine hiking trails, 875 picnic tables, a limited number of picnic pavilions for rental, and five boat launch sites. At the interpretive center, a checklist is available for birdwatchers and a brochure on the geology awaits geology buffs. The road system within the park forms a 14-mile loop popular for sightseeing. At the eastern end of the park is Gull Point Natural Area. It is a 319-acre preserve for nesting and migrating shore and wading birds. This area is closed to all public use from April 1 through November 30. The Perry Monument here honors Commodore Oliver Hazard Perry whose fleet defeated the British in the Battle of Lake Erie during the War of 1812. The park is open all year and there is no admission charge.

2. ERIE HISTORICAL MUSEUM & PLANETARIUM
356 West 6th St., Erie, PA; 814-871-5790

The planetarium is housed in the museum's 19th-century carriage house. Its theatre features a Spitz A3P projector under a 20' dome with seating for 40 people. Open all year, call ahead for days and times of planetarium shows. There is an admission fee.

3. ERIE ZOO, 423 West 38th St., Erie, PA; 814-864-6272

The Erie Zoo occupies 15 acres and houses more than 300 animals. Nearby is a picnic area with plenty of parking. Available are refreshment stands with seated eating areas, a safari land train ride, a children's zoo, a gift shop, and educational programs for all ages. The zoo is open all year and there is an admission fee.

4. ASBURY WOODS NATURE CENTER
4105 Asbury Rd., Erie, PA; 814-835-5356

This is an environmental learning center for all ages, offering special events throughout the year. There are more than three miles of hiking trails, including a barrier-free boardwalk; exhibits, and a giftshop. The center is open all year; no admission charge.

Please call ahead to verify days and times of operations & events

5. CASSADAGA-CONEWANGO WATERWAY

Cassadaga Creek: South Stockton to Levant,
Conewango Creek: Kennedy to Warren County line (PA)

Both Cassadaga Creek and Conewango Creek are Allegany River tributaries and were used by Native Americans, explorers and early settlers. Today they provide anglers with good fishing for muskellunge, bass, and panfish, and area trappers still harvest beaver, muskrat, and mink in accordance with NYS DEC rules and regulations.

These creeks offer generally easy canoeing, but each year large trees topple into the water and can be obstructive. The water level changes throughout the year particularly on Cassadaga Creek. In dry years it is sometimes necessary to walk beside the canoe.

There are several access points and parking areas constructed by the Chautauqua County Parks Commission. Adirondack-style lean-to shelters have been built on a county-owned island in Conewango Creek and on several county-owned acres on the west bank of the Cassadaga Creek. Other lands are privately-owned and should be respected.

6. WESTSIDE OVERLAND TRAIL, Summerdale-Panama

A part of the National Trail System, this 25-mile hiking trail begins at Summerdale and winds through State Reforestation Areas, Chautauqua County land, privately-owned land, and ends in Panama. Along the trail are two camping lean-tos with privies. Hikers are requested to carry out everything they bring in.

7. EASTSIDE OVERLAND TRAIL, County Route 72, Dunkirk

This 19-mile trail begins at County Route 72 in the Canadaway Creek National Wildlife Management Area (see #12) and ends at 28th Creek Road near Gerry. The trail winds through the wildlife management area, NYS Reforestation Areas, Chautauqua County land, and privately-owned property. Hikers are requested to carry out everything they carry in.

Please call ahead to verify days and times of operations & events

8. PANAMA ROCKS SCENIC PARK
11 Rock Hill Road, Panama; 716-782-2845

Panama Rocks is reputed to be the world's most extensive out-crop of glacier-cut, oceanic quartz conglomerate; origins: Paleozoic sea islands. A half-mile ridge of massive rocks, some 70' high, is set amidst an old forest. This unique geological wonder includes cliffs, cavernous dens, caves, and hundreds of crevice passageways. Grotesque tree roots snake down cliffs. Self-guided tours and off-trail exploring are permitted; allow at least one hour.

The park is part of an historic private estate. An admission fee is charged; open May to mid-October, 10 am to 5 pm. Park is 5 miles south of Exit 7 of Southern Tier Expressway (NY 17) and 21 miles south of the Seaway Trail.

9. JAMESTOWN AUDUBON NATURE CENTER, 1600 Riverside Rd, Jamestown, NY 14701; 716-569-2345

The Roger Tory Peterson Intrepretive Building is named for the noted bird artist and ornithologist. The interpretive center houses a large collection of Peterson prints, exhibits, and more than 200 mounted birds. The facility offers a children's hands-on discovery room, five miles of hiking trails, cross-country skiing, photography blinds, a 60-tree arboretum, an herb garden, and a gift shop.

The center is open all year: Tuesday-Saturday 10 am - 5 pm; Sundays 1-5 pm. An annual Nature Art show is held around the third weekend in October; call ahead for exact date. Jamestown is about 25 miles south of the Seaway Trail.

10. LAKE ERIE STATE PARK
off U.S. Route 5, Brocton; 716-792-9214

The park is located on 355 acres between U.S. Route 5 and the Lake Erie shore near the village of Brocton, NY. Facilities include 10 cabins, 95 campsites, showers and flush toilets, a picnic area, a 3/4-mile sandy beach, and 40' high bluffs overlooking the lake. There are two hiking trails, each about 1.5 miles in length with an illustrated trail guide for one. The trails are available in winter for cross-country skiing.

Please call ahead to verify days and times of operations & events

11. POINT GRATIOT PARK BEACH, Dunkirk

This is the municipal beach for the City of Dunkirk. It has a sandy beach of several hundred yards, changing room, and rest rooms. Nearby is a grassy picnic area with tables and shelters.

12. CANADAWAY CREEK NATURE SANCTUARY, Dunkirk; 716-546-8030

Canadaway Creek Nature Sanctuary, one of the few green spaces left on the Lake Erie shoreline between Presque Isle, PA, and Buffalo, NY, is owned and managed by The Nature Conservancy. Historically, the area was apparently the site of an Erie Indian fishing village, later taken over by the Senecas of the Iroquois Confederacy.

The sanctuary borders Canadaway Creek at its outlet into Lake Erie. The land area is a typical flood plain covered with low-land deciduous trees of medium height and 9% open field. Wild grape has overgrown many of the trees, killing several by shading their leaves. This land has long been recognized as a major stopover for migrating birds. Dense thickets provide protection for small land birds and the quiet waters and shores of the creek shelter waterfowl and shorebirds. So far, 160+ species of birds have been identified here. Good times to visit are during spring or fall migration. Visitors are encouraged to wear boots.

The mission of The Nature Conservancy, a private, not-for-profit organization committed to the preservation of natural diversity, is to identify, protect, and maintain the best examples of communities, ecosystems, and endangered species in the natural world.

13. SENECA-IROQUOIS NATION MUSEUM
Allegany Indian Reservation, Salamanca; 716-945-1738

This museum features cultural and historic exhibits of the indigenous inhabitants of the region, including prehistoric to contemporary artifacts and art. It is located several miles inland from the Seaway Trail, take Route 17 to Exit 20 for Salamanca.

14. ALLEGANY STATE PARK, Salamanca; 716-354-2182

NYS' largest State Park, this park is a bit inland from the Seaway Trail in Cattaraugus County and includes two lakes, many streams, 21 miles of ski trails, 55 miles of snowmobile/horseback trails, and 70 miles of hiking paths; tent & trailer sites, and cabins.

Please call ahead to verify days and times of operations & events

15. EVANGOLA STATE PARK, Route 5 (Shaw Rd), Irving;
    campgrounds: May-October: 716-549-1760,
    bathhouse: mid-June-Labor Day: 716-549-1050,
    maintenance: October-April: 716-549-1802

This is on Route 5, 27 miles southwest of Buffalo. It is on 733 acres of former farmland on the shore of Lake Erie. Available facilities include picnic tables and shelters, rest rooms, 80 campsites, a natural sand swimming beach with bath house, and special programs and performances.

16. BENNETT BEACH, 8260 Lake Shore Rd, Angola; 716-549-6060

A sandy beach about 22 miles southwest of Buffalo, Bennett Beach is managed by the City of Buffalo Department of Human Services, Parks and Recreation, 716-851-5806. Admission charged.

17. WENDT BEACH, 7676 Old Lake Shore Rd., Derby; 716-947-5660

A sandy beach about 20 miles southwest of Buffalo, Wendt Beach is a beautiful expanse of beach with some foredunes supporting beach grass. There are sometimes lifeguards on duty. Nearby are picnic tables, a playground, and a concession stand. Wendt Beach is owned and managed by Erie County.

18. TIFFT NATURE PRESERVE

1200 Fuhrmann Blvd., Buffalo; 716-896-5200

This is a beautiful natural area on 264 acres just three miles from downtown Buffalo. The preserve is dedicated to conservation and environmental education. Some of the highlights for visitors are five miles of hiking trails, free guided nature walks (call for times), a self-guided nature and fitness trail, a 75-acre freshwater cattail marsh with viewing blinds, a wildflower garden, snowshoe rental for winter hiking, and special seasonal programs, classes and guided tours.

Tifft Nature Preserve, open year'round Tuesday-Sunday dawn to dusk, is associated with the Buffalo Museum of Science. The Visitor Center is open Tuesday-Sunday, 9 am to 5 pm, free admission.

Please call ahead to verify days and times of operations & events

19. Buffalo & Erie County Botanical Gardens
2655 South Park Ave, Buffalo; 716-828-1040

Designed by Frederick Law Olmsted, the Botanical Gardens Conservatory was built in the late 1890s and is listed on the New York State and National Registries of Historic Places. The conservatory occupies about 11 acres which are owned and managed by Erie County. The many highlights of the gardens offer a pleasant and informative way to spend a day.

Among the attractions are the Palm Dome, a 67' high dome housing a magnificent palm collection; a skywalk and waterfall, the only rainforest in western New York; the Cactus House with the best collection of cacti in the northeast; an area set aside for orchids and other tropical flowers; a children's learning garden; and an edible fruit house featuring citrus trees, coffee, pineapple, carob, and pepper plants. In addition, in summer there are beautiful outside shrub and perennial gardens.

The Botanical Gardens are open all year, 9 am-4 pm weekdays, 9-5 on weekends. Call for special events dates and details.

20. Buffalo Museum of Science
1020 Humboldt Parkway, Buffalo; 716-896-5200

The Museum of Science introduces the visitor to the exciting world of natural science through both permanent and temporary exhibits. Administrated by the Buffalo Society of Natural Sciences, the museum was established in 1861. A brochure provided at the museum entrance will guide the visitor through Insect World, the Hall of Space, the Hall of Endangered Species, the Marchand Hall of Wildflowers, the Hall of Invertebrates, Topics in Evolution, the Hall of the Niagara Frontier, the Hall of Early Technology, Dinosaurs and Company, the Savage Hall of Zoology, the Hall of Gems and Minerals, and the Discovery Room for children. Traveling exhibits regularly highlight a particular area of science or world culture.

The Kellogg and Solar Observatories on the museum's 4th floor are open throughout the year with some evening hours. Museum hours at the time of writing: Tuesday-Sunday 10 am to 5 pm; winter Fridays evenings. There is an admission charge.

Please call ahead to verify days and times of operations & events

21. BUFFALO ZOO
300 Parkside Avenue, Buffalo; 716-837-3900

The Buffalo Zoo, the third oldest zoo in the U.S., opened in 1875. Attracting more than a half-million visitors each year, the zoo houses approximately 1,000 animals on 23 acres. New attractions in 1996 included the African Predator exhibit housing the zoo's hyenas. Other attractions are the Lowland Gorilla/African Rain Forest, lion and tiger "habicats," and the World of Wildlife building. Special events are held throughout the year.

The Buffalo Zoo's dedication to education is demonstrated by a children's zoo and special programming as well as its science magnet school which annually teaches 240 children in grades 7 and 8. The Buffalo Science Magnet School is the only school in the country actually situated on the grounds of a zoo.

The zoo's summer hours are Memorial Day-Labor Day, 10 am to 5:30 pm; the rest of the year: daily from 10 am to 4:30 pm. There is an admission charge.

22. BUFFALO RIVER URBAN CANOE TRAIL
Harlem Rd. to Ohio St. Bridge, Buffalo; 315-646-1000

This six-mile water trail on the Buffalo River takes canoeists through natural, urban and industrial sections past historic sites of Iroquois camps, marshes, bird colonies, and sites of Buffalo's industrial heritage.

The natural section is shallow with wildlife viewing opportunities; the urban stretch shows signs of human encroachment by homes and small businesses; the industrial section evidences Buffalo's manufacturing heyday when steel and chemical processing, petroleum refining, grain milling and transportation were active there. Paddling this trail takes about 4 hours one way without wind. The NYS Department of Environmental Conservation (DEC) advises use of life vests and no trespassing on shore.

Copies of the Urban Canoe Trail Guide produced by the DEC are available for the cost of copying and postage from Seaway Trail, Inc., P.O. Box 660, Sackets Harbor, NY 13685; 1-800-SEAWAY-T.

Please call ahead to verify days and times of operations & events

23. BEAVER ISLAND STATE PARK
   off I-190, Grand Island; 716-773-3271

This 952-acre park is located at the southern tip of Grand Island in the Niagara River. It has a nature center, an 18-hole golf course, a marina with 18 slips, a one-half mile long sandy beach with bathhouse, picnic tables and shelters, and rest rooms. The park is open year'round with cross-country skiing, ice fishing, and sledding as winter activities. Special programs and performances are offered throughout the year.

24. BUCKHORN ISLAND STATE PARK, I-190 at N. Grand Island Bridge,
   Grand Island; 716-773-3271

This 896-acre nature preserve is at the north end of Grand Island in the Niagara River. It has unmarked trails for hiking but no visitor center nor other facilities. Guided nature trail hikes are arranged through the Niagara Frontier State Parks Interpretive Office at 716-278-1728.

Please call ahead to verify days and times of operations & events

25. CAVE OF THE WINDS, Niagara Reservation State Park, Niagara Falls; 716-278-1730

Goat Island is in the Niagara Reservation State Park between the Horseshoe and the American Falls. Terrapin Point, at the island's west end, is an excellent location for viewing the Horseshoe Falls and upriver rapids. Goat Island is the starting point for the Cave of the Winds trip to the base of spectacular Bridal Veil Falls. There is a fee for the trip and for parking at the western end of the island. The east end parking lot is free. This is a wonderful place for a quiet walk, a picnic, or jogging around the measured mile. Visits here are included in the NYS Master Pass for April to October.

26. NIAGARA RESERVATION STATE PARK, Prospect Park, Niagara Falls; 716-278-1770; 278-1796

The visitor center here is surrounded by Great Lakes Gardens with kinetic water sculptures, exhibits, a tourist information center, gift shop, snack bar, and restrooms. The wide screen thrill film "Niagara Wonders" can be viewed in the Festival Theatre for a fee. The New York State Park Observation Tower at Prospect Point offers an outstanding view of the Horseshoe Falls, American Falls, and the upper rapids. This is a great spot to enjoy a rainbow in the morning mist or see the falls illuminated in colored lights at night. From the observation tower, visitors may take an elevator to the NYS Viewmobile or embark on a Maid of the Mist boat tour of the falls. There is a fee for each of these tours. NYS Master Passes are available at the Visitor Center.

27. WINTERGARDEN, 300 Rainbow Blvd., Niagara Falls; 716-286-4940

This is a botanical garden of 7,000 tropical plants in a 107' high glass-framed greenhouse. This facility is a pleasant horticultural surprise amid the commercial activity of downtown Niagara Falls. The Wintergarden is often used for wedding ceremonies and is beautifully decorated during the annual Festival of Lights from Thanksgiving to New Year's Eve. It is open daily throughout the year 8 am to 11 pm; no entrance fee.

Please call ahead to verify days and times of operations & events

28. SCHOELLKOPF GEOLOGICAL MUSEUM

Robert Moses Parkway North, Niagara Falls; 716-278-1780; tours: 716-278-1728

This facility is located on state park land a few hundred yards north of the American Falls. Exhibits and a multiscreen theatre presentation give the five-million-year-old geological history of the Niagara area. A panoramic view of the Falls and Niagara Gorge can be seen from the observation area. A geologic garden at the rear of the museum displays rock structures extracted from the gorge. Park interpretive staff conduct guided tours on trails along the rim of the gorge and more strenuous ones that descend into the gorge to the edge of the rushing Niagara River. The museum is open year'round but is closed Monday through Wednesday during the winter months. This site is included in the NYS Master Pass for April to October.

29. AQUARIUM OF NIAGARA

701 Whirlpool St., Niagara Falls; 716-285-3575

At the Aquarium of Niagara, the visitor can embark on a journey through the waters of the world from the Great Lakes to the world's oceans. Great Lakes exhibitry includes displays on Lake Erie, Lake Ontario, the Niagara River ecosystem, and the lamprey eel's relationship to sportfishing.

There are more than 1500 aquatic animals and the largest collection of freshwater game fish in New York State here. Also seen are sharks, piranha, river otters sea horses, and lion fish. The Aquarium of Niagara is one of only 10 North American sites to house a colony of endangered Peruvian penguins. Sea lion demonstrations are offered every 90 minutes. On alternating days there are shark or otter feedings with an educational Meet the Keeper program. An observation deck gives a commanding view of the Falls and Niagara River Gorge. It's just a short stroll to the Falls or the Viewmobile.

A new feature at the Aquarium are Dive Adventures in the main salt water tank with California sea lions. This special opportunity is by reservation only. Call for details. The Aquarium is open year'round, 9 am to 5 pm daily and until 7 pm Memorial Day-Labor Day; admission charge, NYS Master Pass accepted, free parking, and handicapped access.

Please call ahead to verify days and times of operations & events

30. WHIRLPOOL STATE PARK
Robert Moses Parkway, Niagara Falls; 716-285-3893

This park is about two and a half miles north of the Schoellkopf Geological Museum on the Robert Moses Parkway. Its 109 acres extend along the rim of the Niagara Gorge 265 feet above the river. Several observation points provide excellent views of the gorge, rapids, and Whirlpool including the cable car that crosses the Whirlpool between stations on the Canadian side of the river. There are stairs down the side of the gorge to the Ongiara Trail along the river. The park has picnic tables and rest rooms. It is open year'round.

31. DEVILS HOLE STATE PARK
Robert Moses Parkway, Niagara Falls; 716-285-3893

The park is about three miles north of the City of Niagara Falls on the Robert Moses Parkway. Along the rim of the Niagara Gorge, it offers a magnificent view of the Niagara River and the power-generating facilities on the American side. There are steps leading down the side of the gorge to the river 220' below. The park has picnic tables and rest rooms. It is open all year.

32. EARL W. BRIDGES ARTPARK
Route 18F, Portage Road, Lewiston; 716-754-9000

The 200-acre Artpark is a New York State Park located seven miles north of Niagara Falls on the Niagara River. The main focus of the park is on performing and visual arts. Presentations in the 2,300-seat theater include musicals, international dance companies, and top names of jazz, blues, folk and pop music. Visual arts programming includes classes and workshops in a variety of disciplines. There is also a day camp, Camp Artpark, for children ages 6-12.

For those who wish to enjoy the arts and at the same time indulge their love of nature, there are geologically unique nature trails that wind through woody parklands to the end of the gorge. There is plenty of room for picnicking, bicycling, and fishing. Artpark is open all year but its primary season is during the summer months of June, July and August. There is a charge for activities.

Please call ahead to verify days and times of operations & events

33. Joseph Davis State Park, Robert Moses Parkway or Rte. 18F, Lewiston; 716-754-4596

This park occupies 358 acres of land that was formerly a fruit farm. Among the activities offerred here are picnicking, hiking, fishing, swimming, and golfing. The picnic area has tables and shelters with nearby rest rooms. There is a 1.5 miles nature trail where many native plants and animals can be seen. A fishing pond in the park contains largemouth bass and sunfish. An entrance fee is required for the pool. An unusual feature of the park is an 18-hole disc golf course. A handicapped-accessible fishing dock on the Niagara River is available with nearby parking.

The park is open year'round and winter activities are cross-country skiing and snowshoeing. Special programs and performances are offered throughout the year.

34. Niagara Power Project Visitors Center
5777 Lewiston Rd, Lewiston; 716-285-3211

This visitors center is part of the 5th largest power project in the world. The center offers educational exhibits, audio-visual shows, computer games and hands-on displays on hydroelectric power production. Fishing enthusiasts can cast their line for salmon, trout and steelhead from a $1 million fishing pier here.

35. Fort Niagara State Park, Robert Moses Parkway or Rte. 18F, Youngstown; Park: 716-745-7273,
Old Fort Niagara: 716-745-7611

On 240 acres at the mouth of the Niagara River, the park has a hiking trail, picnic areas with tables, barbecue grills, shelters, play areas for children, tennis, soccer, snowshoeing, cross-country skiing, snowmobiling, and a sledding hill. Two boat launches provide access to the river. A New York State Historic Site, Fort Niagara is located at the western tip of the park. Living history demonstrations, re-enactments and special events are featured at the fort operated by the Old Fort Niagara Association on a non-profit basis. The park and fort are open year'round. Old Fort Niagara lighthouse, dating to 1781, is one of more than 20 historic lights on the Seaway Trail. The fort has a year'round fee; the park has a summer season usage fee.

Please call ahead to verify days and times of operations & events

36. FOUR MILE CREEK STATE CAMPGROUND, Robert Moses Parkway (Lake Rd), Youngstown; 716-745-3802, 800-456-CAMP

On July 6, 1759, at the mouth of Four Mile Creek, 2200 British soldiers and 900 Iroquois warriors landed to begin the siege of Fort Niagara. Eighteen days later, as a turning point in the French and Indian War, the French-occupied fort was surrendered. Four Mile Creek State Campground is located on 248 acres of this historic site. There are 329 campsites spread throughout this acreage. 138 sites have electric hookups. Laundry facilities and hot showers are available as are hiking trails, play areas, and freshwater fishing. The campsite opens in mid-April and closes mid-October.

37. WILSON-TUSCARORA STATE PARK
Route 18, Lake Road, Wilson; 716-751-6361

This park consists of 390 acres of mature woods, open meadows, and marshlands. A four-mile hiking trail is available for those who enjoy seeing plants and animals in their native habitats. Scenic views of Lake Ontario can be enjoyed from the picnic area which has tables and grills. This is the place for anglers who like fishing derbies. They are offerred in the spring, summer, and fall. During the winter months, trails are open to cross-country skiing and snowshoeing.

38. GOLDEN HILL STATE PARK, 9691 Lower Lake Road, Barker; 716-795-3885, 800-456-CAMP

This park consists of 510 acres of which 377 are on land and 133 are under water. Facilities and features offered are campsites, historic Thirty Mile Point Lighthouse, hiking trails, picnic shelters, and a boat launch ramp. Two very informative self-guiding trail guides are available: "Guide to Thirty Mile Point Lighthouse" and "Shoreline Nature Trail Guide." The park is open in winter for cross-country skiing and snowshoeing.

"January Thaw," a limited edition print by artist Ron Kleiber, features red-head ducks near Thirty Mile Point Lighthouse. Sales of the print benefit the Seaway Trail Foundation, P.O. Box 660, Sackets Harbor, NY 13685. Ron, whose home and studio border the Iroquois National Wildlife Refuge (see #40), has also painted NYS Duck, Delaware Trout, Florida Wild Turkey, Mississippi and Ohio Duck U.S. postage stamps.

Please call ahead to verify days and times of operations & events

NYS' SEAWAY TRAIL CENTRAL SEGMENT:
ORLEANS COUNTY

39. INSTITUTE FOR ENVIRONMENTAL LEARNING
12398 Platten Rd., Lyndonville; 716-765-2084

Located on a 14-acre farm in rural Orleans County, the Institute features a collection of common and endangered predators. Programs, with follow-up activities, are offered by the Institute at schools and to school groups on topics such as Predators Role in Ecology, Bird Migration, Pesticides: Invisible Killer of Wildlife, Hunting and Trapping in Wildlife Management, and Photographing Wildlife and Nature.

The Institute has the only socialized wolf pack in the eastern U.S. This means that they are maintained under managed conditions, not that they are tame. This pack provides an excellent opportunity for photography and for observing wolf behavior. Other rehabilitated or captive-born predators featured at the time of my visit included two mountain lions, two bald eagles, and an assortment of hawks and owls.

Visits by the public are available by appointment only by calling 716-765-2084. There is a modest fee for each visit.

40. IROQUOIS NATIONAL WILDLIFE REFUGE
off Route 63 on Casey Rd, Alabama; 716-948-5445

Nearly 11,000 acres of marshland, wooded swamp, wet meadows, pasture, and cropland constitute the Iroquois National Wildlife Refuge. The western half of Oak Orchard Swamp is within the refuge. The eastern half of the swamp is a New York State Wildlife Management Area. The combined federal and state lands provide almost 20,000 acres of prime waterfowl habitat, managed primarily for migrating waterfowl. The Iroquois Refuge encourages birdwatching, hiking, canoeing, nature study, photography, cross-country skiing, and bicycling.

The Refuge maintains three nature trails: Onondaga, Kanyoo, and Swallow Hollow, four overlooks, and photography blinds for

Please call ahead to verify days and times of operations & events

visitor use. The best time to observe bird migration is during the first two weeks in April and from the second week in September through the first week in October. Birdwatching is best March to November with 266 species having been identified on the refuge. During March, bald eagles can sometimes be observed building their nests. Thirty-three mammal species have been recorded along with reptiles, fish, and amphibians.

The visitor center on Casey Road is open 8 am - 4 pm Monday-Friday. It is also open on weekends during spring migration. The Iroquois Refuge is about 16 miles south of the Seaway Trail.

41. ORLEANS COUNTY MARINE PARK, Lake Ontario State Parkway & Rte. 98, north of Albion; 716-589-6145

This park is located on 11 acres along the scenic Oak Orchard River. Facilities include picnic grounds, fishing access with cleaning station, scenic overlook walk with handicapped access, temporary docking area, yearly boat slip rentals (72 with electric), and restrooms open Memorial Day to late October.

42. COBBLESTONE SOCIETY MUSEUM COMPLEX
14393 Ridge Rd., Albion; 716-589-9013 or 716-589-9510

A 22-mile stretch of the Ridge Road between Childs in Orleans County and Parma in Monroe County offers a look at least 21 examples of cobblestone architecture. The use of cobblestones combined with mortar dates back to the Romans and their use of beach flint in England. The development of cobblestone masonry in western New York began about the same time as the construction of the Erie Canal, completed in 1825. The Cobblestone Era is usually dated 1820s to 1860s.

There are two kinds of cobbles: glacial laid or field cobbles, and water-laid cobbles left here after Lake Iroquois receded back to its present-day size of Lake Ontario. During the time of cobblestone architecture's height along the Seaway Trail, more than 700 cobblestone buildings were built along the southern shore of Lake Ontario. Orleans and Monroe Counties each have about 100 such structures. Niagara County, to the west, has about 50 cobblestone structures. Wayne County, farther east, has nearly 200, many found along Route

Please call ahead to verify days and times of operations & events

42. Cobblestone Society Museum Complex (con't)

104A and the Ridge Road through Red Creek, the coastal townships of Huron and Sodus, following the trail to Lake Road into the Town of Williamson and its historic hamlet of Pultneyville.

The Village of Albion in Orleans County has 34 buildings around its Courthouse Square which are listed in the National Historic Register of Historic Places. The Cobblestone Society Museum, two miles north of Albion, stewards three cobblestone buildings and seven frame buildings. Included are the first cobblestone church in North America (1834), a cobblestone parsonage, and a cobblestone school as well as blacksmith, print and harness shops, and Farmer's Hall containing some 300 farming artifacts and a collection of mounted birds of Western New York.

The museum is open mid-June through Labor Day, except Mondays; and September-October: Sundays, 1-5. Tour groups are accepted by appointment in May, September and October. There is a fee.

43. Lakeside Beach State Park
Lake Ontario State Parkway, Waterport; 716-682-5246

The 743 acres of the park have 274 campsites overlooking Lake Ontario. The shoreline in the region has high, steep banks with a cobble beach so there is no swimming. All the campsites have electric hookups and camping is available from late April to late October. Also available are playing fields and a playground, picnic areas with tables and fireplaces, camp store, laundromat, and recreation programs during summer months. The park is open all winter for hiking, cross-country skiing, and snowmobiling. Nearby is Oak Orchard State Marine Park on both sides of the Oak Orchard River with seven boat launches and 10 boat slips. This park is 35 miles west of Rochester on the Lake Ontario shoreline.

44. Erie Canal Heritage Trail

The Erie County Heritage Trail begins at the Orleans County western line and follows the New York State Barge Canal across Orleans and Monroe Counties. The trail essentially forms a 70-mile long New York State Park. This trail park is ideal for hiking, biking, and cross-country skiing. It is eight feet wide with some paved and some gravel surfaces.

Please call ahead to verify days and times of operations & events

Canal parks are found in the villages of Albion and Medina. The trail has access to boat launches near Bates Road, Fruit Avenue, Brooks Avenue, Westfall Road, Jefferson Road, Clover Street, and Marsh Road. For biking and hiking there are 60 access points near major thoroughfares. Boaters can view beautiful greenways and agricultural settings between villages. Mule-drawn packet boat tours are also available.

45. HAMLIN BEACH STATE PARK

Lake Ontario State Parkway, Hamlin; 716-964-2462

With its 1100 acres, Hamlin Beach State Park is the only developed camping facility in Monroe County. There are 264 tent and trailer campsites available from the last week in April through Columbus Day. More than one-half mile of swimming beach sometimes has lifeguards on duty. Five picnic areas provide tables and four enclosed shelters. The Yanty Creek Nature Trail is associated with an Environmental Education Center at the eastern end of the park. The trail provides a view of the 200-acre Yanty Marsh Environmental Area. About a mile in length, the nature trail is a self-guided, informational trail with large print signs along the path. The park office is open year'round. Hamlin Beach State Park is 25 miles west of the City of Rochester.

46. HIGHLAND PARK

Highland Ave. & South Goodman St., Rochester;
716-256-4950

A Monroe County Park of 150 acres, Highland Park was designed by Frederick Law Olmstead as Rochester's first park in 1888 to appear as a natural occurrence of trees, shrubs, and flowers. It is actually a completely planned and planted arboretum or "tree garden."

In addition to the 1200 lilac shrubs that comprise the 22-acre springtime hillside display along Highland Avenue, the park boasts a Japanese Maple collection; 35 varieties of sweet-smelling magnolias; a barberry collection; a rock garden featuring dwarf evergreens; 700 varieties of rhododendron, azaleas, mountain laurel, and andromeda; horse chestnut, spring bulbs, wildflowers, and a large number of rare trees.

One of the events that Highland Park is best known for is the annual May Lilac Festival. Rochester shows its most elegant floral finery during this spectacular festival which also includes musical and dramatic entertainment, foot races, an arts & crafts show, and numerous other activities. The park is open year'round.

Please call ahead to verify days and times of operations & events

47. THE LAMBERTON CONSERVATORY
Highland Park, Rochester; 716-244-8079

The conservatory is housed in a recently renovated 1911 building in Highland Park (see #46). Exhibits change five times a year and feature seasonal floral displays that might not otherwise survive Rochester's non-tropical climate. The Main Dome protects the Tropical Forest Display and other climate-controlled rooms contain collections of exotic plants, desert plants, house plants, and plants such as banana and coffee trees.

The conservatory is open Tuesday-Sunday 10 am to 6 pm; Wednesday evenings to 8 pm.

48. THE GARDEN CENTER OF ROCHESTER
Highland Park, Rochester; 716-473-5130

Headquarters for the center is historic Warner Castle, a Gothic-style residence that was formerly the house of Rochester attorney and newspaper editor Horatio Gates Warner. A non-profit educational organization, the Garden Center collects and disseminates horticultural information. Its display gardens include a sunken garden, a shady border, rock garden, country side garden, day lily bed, old-fashioned rose bed, miniature rose bed, fern bed, and a 13th-century herb garden.

The Garden Center is located in Highland Park (see #46).

49. DURAND EASTMAN PARK, Lakeshore Blvd. or Kings Highway, Rochester; 716-256-4950

A Monroe County Park of 965 acres, Durand Eastman Park is between the Genesee River and Irondequoit Bay with a 5,000' Lake Ontario waterfront. Because of its many mature plant specimens, this park and Highland Park make up the Monroe County Arboretum.

The park provides an 18-hole golf course, and hiking trails, and picnic shelters with tables and grills. In winter, cross-country skiers find hilly terrain to conquer.

Please call ahead to verify days and times of operations & events

50. ROCHESTER MUSEUM AND SCIENCE CENTER
657 East Ave. at Goodman St., Rochester; 716-271-4320

In a 12-acre park-like setting, the Science Center consists of the Rochester Museum, Strasenburgh Planetarium, Cumming Nature Center, Gannet School of Science and Man, and the Eisenhart Auditorium. Upstate New York's multi-faceted past are revealed at the Rochester Museum through permanent and changing exhibits on the natural and cultural heritage of the Finger Lakes and lower Genesee regions. Always on view are large colorful dioramas of area flora and fauna, and of the fossil seas from 300 million years ago.

The Museum Research Library has approximately 1.5 million objects which are used to interpret the region's history, natural history, and ethnic diversity. Exhibits include "Dinosaurs! Goin' North," "Big Bugs," and "Mazes after the Dinosaurs: The Age of Mammals and Ice."

The museum is open year'round, Monday-Saturday 9 am - 5 pm, Sundays and holidays from 12 noon to 5 pm. There is an admission charge.

51. RMSC STRASENBURGH PLANETARIUM
657 East Avenue, Rochester; 716-271-1880

For the nearly 200,000 visitors each year the world of science and theater unite in this unique planetarium environment to make possible anything in the universe. The Zeiss Mark VI Projector, hundreds of other projectors, and an astonishing sound system are all under computer control, waiting to transport the visitor through time and space. Light pollution is banished at the push of a button and the night sky becomes visible as ancient space, witnessing the birth of a solar system, walking the strange soil of alien worlds or journeying across the galaxy. A visit to the Star Theater is a visit to the entire cosmos.

There is a charge for admission to the planetarium shows. The planetarium is part of the Rochester Museum and Science Center (see #50).

Please call ahead to verify days and times of operations & events

52. CUMMING NATURE CENTER

6472 Gulick Road, Naples; 716-374-6160

Naples is in Ontario County and is more than 40 miles south of the Seaway Trail. It is listed here because it is a part of the Rochester Museum and Science Center. The nature center has six miles of thematic trails that wind their way through 900 acres, passing a 35-acre beaver pond, a fully operational sawmill, an 18th-century homestead, and outdoor art galleries. There are five trails that begin at the Visitors Center which is a combination reception area, multimedia theater, and a gallery for wildlife art exhibits and environmentally-related displays. The center also has a snack bar, gift shop, rest rooms, and houses a variety of birds, mammals, and reptiles used in educational programs. Winter activities include cross-country skiing and snowshoeing.

The Cumming Nature Center has been designated a National Environmental Study Area by the National Park Service. The center is open Wednesday-Sunday, 9 am - 5 pm; closed mid-November until the Wednesday after Christmas.

53. SENECA PARK ZOO

2222 St. Paul Blvd., Rochester; 716-467-9453

Seneca Park is a Monroe County Park of 297 acres designed by Frederick Law Olmstead. The park was formed to preserve three miles of forested river gorge and features picnic areas, hiking trails, open fields, spectacular views of the Genesee River, and playground. The Seneca Park Zoo was created here in 1894. The zoo has more than 350 animals representing more than 140 species. Popular features are the polar bears and the rare Siberian tigers and snow leopards. The tigers, leopards and many other animals at Seneca Park Zoo are part of the Species Survival Plan. New exhibits include the Genesee Trail for native species and the Rocky Coasts of the World exhibit (1997) with polar bears, black-footed penguins, California sea lions, snowy owls, reindeer and Arctic foxes.

The Zoo is open every day of the year from 10 am to 4 pm except for summer weekends and holidays when hours are extended to 6 pm. Parking is free; there is an admission fee.

Please call ahead to verify days and times of operations & events

54. GENESEE VALLEY PARK

Elmwood Ave./East River Rd/Crittenden Rd, Rochester;
716-256-4950

As an 800-acre Monroe County Park along the eastern bank of the Genesee River, Genesee Valley Park features two 18-hole golf courses, soccer and cricket fields, and seven softball diamonds. There are hiking and biking trails that pass through picturesque riverside forest wilderness. Picnic tables and shelters are available for family outings.

Genesee Valley Park West is a City of Rochester Park of 79 acres on the western bank of the Genesee River across from Genesee Valley Park. Footbridges and Elmwood Avenue Bridge connect the two parks. The west park has a public swimming pool, playing fields, tenniscourts, an ice skating rink, and canoe rentals. Both parks are open year'round.

55. THE GENESEE RIVER TRAIL, Rochester; 716-428-6770

Beginning at the intersection with the Erie Canal Heritage Trail, the Genesee River Trail follows the shoreline of the river for a distance of 4.3 miles. The trail begins on the west side of the river, crosses to the east side by the Ford Street Bridge, and continues on the east side to its northern terminus on South Avenue. The hard surface of the trail makes it suitable for biking as well as hiking, jogging, or just plain strolling. The East Bank and West Bank River Trails parallel the Genesee River Trail on the other side of the river.

56. THE FALLS OF THE GENESEE RIVER, Driving Park Avenue, Center at High Falls, Rochester; 716-325-2030

Two spectacular water falls can be observed on the Genesee River as it flows through the City of Rochester. In a different era these provided the power that made Rochester the milling center of central New York. It was once called the Flour City. Later the emphasis on flowers and flowering shrubs resulted in the very appropriate name Flower City. The lower falls are on the three-acre Lower Falls Park. This small park on the west bank offers a beautiful vista of the river tumbling down 96' of steep rock face. The park can be entered from Driving Park Avenue.

Please call ahead to verify days and times of operations & events

At the upper or high falls the Genesee River plunges over an 84' escarpment. The falls is the centerpiece for the Center at High Falls. The Center offers exhibits, video and multi-imaging slide media, "action" murals, special events and programs, and self-guided tours. This Urban Cultural Park is in a city park of five acres at 60 Browns Race.

"River of Light: A Celebration of Rochester and the Genesee" is a spectacular music and light show that bathes the High Falls in vivid hues at dusk as a prelude to the moment when a 500' section of the gorge wall becomes a screen for a dazzling laser light and sound presentation. The laser show starts at dusk Wednesday-Saturday from late June to early September, on some fall weekends and for special holiday shows. Call for exact dates.

57. MAPLEWOOD ROSE GARDEN PARK
Driving Park & Lake Avenue, Rochester; 716-428-6770

The heavy, intoxicating scent of roses fills the air around Maplewood Rose Garden throughout most of the summer months. The approximately 3,500 roses that bloom in the park represent 250 varieties, including hybrid tea roses, and smaller collections of grandifloras, hybrid perpetuals, florabunda, and shrub roses. Peak blooming time usually occurs around the third week of June and flowering continues until the first frost.

58. ONTARIO BEACH PARK
Lake or Beach Avenue, Rochester; 716-256-4950

Accessible from Lake or Beach Avenue, the 39-acre Monroe County Park on the shore of Lake Ontario is in the northwest corner of the City of Rochester. The beach area, several hundred feet wide and more than one-half mile long, is one of the best natural sand beaches along the Great Lakes. The 1905 Dentzel Menageries Carousel provides a turn-of-the-century flavor to the park, which also includes a performance pavilion that often features the County Parks Band. The park offers a year'round public boat launch, a lighted fishing pier, soccer and softball fields, six picnic shelters, volleyball courts, a food concession, a bathhouse, and an ice skating rink. Lifeguards are on duty at the beach during summer months.

Please call ahead to verify days and times of operations & events

59. Mendon Ponds Park

Route 6 or Pittsford-Mendon Center Road, Pittsford;
716-256-4950; Nature Center: 716-334-3780

A Monroe County Park of 2,514 acres in the southeastern portion of the county, this is the largest of the county parks. It offers a variety of recreational opportunities including hiking, bridle and cross-country ski trails, fishing areas, a cartop boat launch, picnic shelters and lodges, many informal picnic areas, two softball fields, playgrounds, and a group camping area.

The park is a living natural history museum of glacial geology. It was named to the National Registry of Natural Landmarks in 1969. Many of the "ponds" that give the park its name are really kettles, roughly circular depressions formed by the melting of buried blocks of ice left behind by the retreating glacier. "Devil's Bathtub" is the most prominent and well known of the kettles. Round Pond and Lost Pond are also water-filled kettles.

Most of the glacial formations found in the park are the result of the melting of the Wisconsin ice sheet, the last of four major ice sheets to cover the area in the last million years. The park's Nature Center provides maps and displays of the glacial formations to guide visitors in search of ancient landmarks. Mendon Pond's glacial geology is best appreciated in the fall, winter, and early spring when foliage does not hide its features. The park is open year'round and is 10 miles south of the City of Rochester.

60. North Ponds Park, Route 104 between Holt Road and
North Avenue, Webster; 716-872-4150

A Town of Webster Park of 55 acres, North Ponds Park is a scenic and peaceful retreat along a busy road. The park features bike paths, boating, swimming, picnic and fishing areas, jogging and hiking trails. Try a leisurely stroll on well-marked trails around the pond.

61. Webster Park, Lake & Holt Rds., Webster; 716-256-4950

This park encompasses 550 acres of rolling hills with scenic views of Lake Ontario, picnic shelters, tennis courts, hiking, bridle and skiing trails, and a fishing pier 10 miles northeast of the City of Rochester. A family campground accommodates tents and trailers.

Please call ahead to verify days and times of operations & events

62. THOUSAND ACRE SWAMP SANCTUARY
Jackson Rd, Penfield; 716-546-8030

The sanctuary, managed by the Thousand Acre Swamp Preservation Committee for The Nature Conservancy (see entry #12), is centrally located north of Atlantic Avenue with access from Jackson Road. The sanctuary covers about 350 acres, the swamp is about 800 acres in total size. It includes a variable and diversified number of habitats. Analysis of fossilized pollen from a five foot core of bottomland muck has shown that the swamp originated as a shallow pond or bay at the end of the last ice age 10-12,000 years ago. The management committee has established a number of marked trails for the benefit of visitors. A 670' boardwalk over the wet swamp is a popular feature.

Guided nature hikes led by volunteers and free to the public are held frequently on weekend from April through October. Some of the topics of these walks have been Migrating Spring Birds, Evening in the Swamp, Warm-Blooded Swamp Mammals, Spring Wildflowers, Trees and Shrubs, Summer Stars over the Swamp, Soils and Geology, and Summer Wildflowers.

lilacs

Please call ahead to verify days and times of operations & events

WAYNE AND CAYUGA COUNTIES,
NYS' SEAWAY TRAIL

64. CHIMNEY BLUFFS STATE PARK, East Bay Rd., Town of Huron

This is an undeveloped state park of several hundred acres on the shoreline of Lake Ontario. A one-mile hiking trail loop begins at a poorly defined parking lot. The trail winds along the top of 150' high bluffs that stretch for half a mile along the lake shore. The bluff is a glacial ridge eroded by wind, rain, and waves into sharp ridges and peaks with steep valleys. These provide the geology buff with an opportunity to study the sand, clay, gravel, and boulder mixture that makes up the glacial moraine deposit. There are no facilities and no camping here. Visitors should carry out everything they carry in.

65. MONTEZUMA NATIONAL WILDLIFE REFUGE
3395 Route 5 & 20 East, Seneca Falls

The refuge, established in 1937, contains 6,432 acres of widely diversified habitat, from extensive marshes to upland hardwood forests. These habitats are managed to provide a healthy, self-sustaining population of many wildlife species including mammals, resident birds, reptiles, amphibians, and insects normally found in central New York.

Located in the middle of one of the most active flight lanes in the Atlantic Flyway, the refuge provides resting, feeding, and nesting habitats for waterfowl and other migratory birds. Features at the refuge are a visitor center with exhibits, rest rooms, an observation deck and tower, a 3.5 mile self-guided auto tour providing visitors with an opportunity to observe and photograph wildlife from their cars, and Esker Brook Trail, a two-mile walking trail.

Snow, ice and poor road conditions generally keep the auto tour road closed during the winter and early spring months. The refuge is open year'round during daylight hours. The visitor center is staffed on summer weekends and some hours at other times of year. During the winter months the Auto Tour Trail and the hiking trail are open for cross-country skiing and snowshoeing. Since this is a National Wildlife Refuge, collecting, disturbing, injuring, or damaging plants or animals is prohibited. Montezuma National Wildlife Refuge is about 15 miles south of the Seaway Trail.

Please call ahead to verify days and times of operations & events

66. CANANDAIGUA OUTLET CANOE TRIP, Manchester

Put canoes in the water at Manchester where New York State Route 96 crosses Canandaigua Outlet. The river runs eastward through Ontario County then north through Wayne County to Lyons where it empties into the Barge Canal. The current is moderate and there are access points along the route. Manchester is about 20 miles south of the Seaway Trail.

67. ENTRY TO THE FINGER LAKES REGION; 315-946-5470, 800-527-6510

New York State Routes 21, 88, 14, 414, 89, 38, and 34 offer access from the Seaway Trail to the natural beauty of the Finger Lakes Region, ranked in nationwide destinations worth traveling a long distance to visit by Rand McNally's Vacation Places Rated.

This region is also one of only 17 "unforgettable American road trips" featured in the new volume of Great American Drives published by US News and World Report and the Automobile Association of America.

In addition to swimming, fishing, and boating on the lakes, natural history-oriented sites to visit include Robert Treman, Fillmore Glen, Taughannock Falls, Letchworth and Watkins Glen State Parks; Sonnenberg Gardens & Mansion; the Johnson Museum of Art at Cornell University; Buttermilk Falls; Finger Lakes National Forest; and Tioga Gardens and Conservatory. For more info, contact the Wayne County Office of Public Information at 315-946-5470, 800-527-6510.

68. FAIR HAVEN BEACH STATE PARK
Route 104A, Fair Haven; 315-947-5205

This state park of 865 acres on the shore of Lake Ontario features 191 campsites (44 electric), 32 cabins, a wide sandy beach with bath-house, picnic pavilions, self-guided nature trails, playground, playing fields, picnic areas with tables and fireplaces, concession stand, boat launching ramp, and a camper recreation program. Campground is open mid-April to early November. Hikers, cross-country skiers, and snowmobilers can use the park all winter; six cabins are available with wood heat.

Please call ahead to verify days and times of operations & events

69. CAYUGA COUNTY TRAIL, Fair Haven to Cato

This 15-mile trail begins at Fair Haven and follows an abandoned railroad bed to Cato. An additional segment from Port Byron to Centerport is part of New York State's Canal Park System. This trail is ideal for hiking, snowmobiling, and cross-country skiing.

70. DRUMLIN VIEWING OPPORTUNITIES

Drumlins are smooth hills shaped like inverted bowls or teaspoons. They were formed and shaped by glacier movement. The blunt end of the drumlin points in the direction from which the ice was moving. The region between Lake Ontario and the Finger Lakes is one of the largest drumlin fields in the world with more than 10,000 drumlins. NYS Routes 38 and 34 south from the Seaway Trail pass through excellent drumlin country that is also beautiful farming country. See Suggested Reading #22 *Seaway Trail Rocks and Landscapes* for more information on thegeological formation of this region. It is available from Seaway Trail, Inc., P.O. Box 660, Sackets Harbor, NY 13685.

Please call ahead to verify days and times of operations & events

NYS' SEAWAY TRAIL NORTHEASTERN SEGMENT:

OSWEGO COUNTY

71. RICE CREEK FIELD STATION
Johnson Road, Oswego; 315-342-0961

The field station is a teaching and research unit of the State University of New York College at Oswego. It is located about one mile south of the Seaway Trail on Johnson Road. The station is surrounded by several hundred acres of woodland, successional fields, meadows, and wetlands. Four well-marked and well-kept nature trails provide the visitor with easy access to these areas. Each trail can be walked in less than one hour. The Wildflower Trail, the shortest of four, loops several times through a small, wooded area near the main building and features woodland wildflowers.

A 26-acre pond offers an opportunity for observing aquatic plants, ducks, geese, herons, muskrats, beavers, and turtles. The highlight of the main building is a viewing gallery where visitors can see the pond and hear the electronically-transmitted sounds of an undisturbed aquatic ecosystem. Rice Creek offers a variety of lectures, workshops, and field trips for the general public throughout the year. Cross-country skiing and snowshoeing are favorite winter activities on the trails. Motor vehicles are prohibited on the trails as is collecting. Rice Creek Field Station is open year'round from 9 am to 4:30 pm Monday-Friday, and sometimes on weekends.

72. CURTISS-GALE WILDLIFE MANAGEMENT AREA
State Route 57, Fulton; 607-753-3095

This small wildlife area of about 45 acres is located a mile or two south of the City of Fulton, bordered on its west side by the Oswego River and on the east by New York State Route 57. On the north and south sides it is bordered by privately-owned land. This parcel of land was given to the state by H. Salem Curtis and Thomas and Ida Gale with the stipulation that it remain forever natural and untouched.

Please call ahead to verify days and times of operations & events

72. CURTISS-GALE WILDLIFE MANAGEMENT AREA (CON'T)

The outstanding features of this area are the very large trees in a stand that may be the best example of a mature climax forest in the county. Trees growing here that are less common in other woodlands of the county are tulip tree, white oak, sassafras, and flowering dogwood. The wildlife area has several trails, one of which enters at the northeast corner, winds through the woods with one branch leading down to the river. This is a wonderful spot for a quiet, peaceful stroll through a beautiful, mature woodland.

73. BEAVER LAKE NATURE CENTER
East Mud Lake Rd, Baldwinsville; 315-638-2519

Beaver Lake Nature Center is a 600-acre park operated by Onondaga County. To get to the center from the Seaway Trail, take NY Route 48, then I-690 toward Baldwinsville to the Route 370 exit, and follow the signs west to the Nature Center. The Nature Center is about 21 miles south of the Seaway Trail with a Visitor Center which includes interpretive exhibits, audio-visual programs, a bird feeding area, information on recent wildlife sightings, and staff members who can answer questions and suggest activities to enhance your visit.

The center's eight trails wind through beautiful woodlands and meadows. Boardwalks safely lead you through delightful wetlands teeming with wildlife. Trail length varies from a short jaunt to the lakeshore to the three-mile lake loop trail. Interpretive signs, telescopes, an observation tower, and a wildlife blind are located at special places along the well-marked trails. Canoes are available for rental during the summer months. Winter activities include cross-country skiing, guided snowshoe hikes, historical ice cutting, and birding tours. Beaver Lake Nature Center is open every day from 7:30 am to dusk. There is a modest vehicle fee.

74. RICHARD A. NOYES SANCTUARY, Nine Mile Point Rd,
New Haven; 315-457-7731, 315-668-8000

This 90-acre sanctuary on Lake Ontario's shore is owned by The Nature Conservancy, but maintained in perpetuity by the Onondaga Audubon Society of Syracuse. To get to the sanctuary from The Seaway Trail, take County Route 29 to Lake Road, turn right and drive

Please call ahead to verify days and times of operations & events

for almost a mile to Nine Mile Point Road, turn left and watch for the large wooden sign on the right at the entrance to the parking lot. The trails are ideal for hiking and nature study, and especially for birdwatching and observing wildflowers.

One arm of the trail system passes along the top of cliffs 30 or more feet high that form the shoreline of Lake Ontario. A large colony of barn swallows nest on these rocky cliffs. The sanctuary is open year'round and many of the trails are suitable for cross-country skiing. Visitors are warned that walking too close to the edge of the lakeside cliffs can be extremely dangerous. Combine a visit here with the annual Fall Wildlife Show at The Energy Center, located next to the Nine Mile Point nuclear facilities on Lake Road. The Onondaga Audubon Society maintains a Bird Hotline at 315-668-8000.

75. Derby Hill Bird Observatory
Sage Creek Rd, Mexico Point; 315-457-7731,
during hawk season (Feb-May): 315-963-8291

Derby Hill is a 50-acre sanctuary owned and operated by the Onondaga Audubon Society of Syracuse. It overlooks the southeastern corner of Lake Ontario and is a strategic place to observe the spring migration of 15 species of hawks regularly seen in eastern North America. Rough-legged hawks, goshawks, and red-tailed hawks begin the season in late February. Red-shouldered hawks and northern harriers appear in early April and the peak flights usually occur April 20-30. The fourth weekend in April is a traditional gathering time for hawk watchers from throughout the Northeast. The Derby Hill Bird Sanctuary is located at the end of Sage Creek Road which intersects the Seaway Trail (State Route 104B) one mile west of the intersection of 104B & State Route 3. The Onondaga Audubon Society maintains a Bird Hotline at 315-668-8000.

76. Selkirk Shores State Park
NYS Route 3, Port Ontario; 315-298-5737

Selkirk Shores is a 980-acre state park at the southern end of the eastern Lake Ontario barrier beach and sand dune system. This system serves to protect inland marshes and ponds from wave erosion, thus preserving these habitats and the plants and animals that live

Please call ahead to verify days and times of operations & events

there. The hiking trails in the park offer an opportunity to observe many species of woodland wildflowers, ferns and mosses as well as beach and sand dune plants.

Facilities offered at the park include 148 campsites (88 electric), 24 cabins, a natural sand swimming beach, picnic areas with tables and fireplaces, playground and playing fields, and a boat launching site. The park is open year'round. Swimming is permitted in summer; trails are available for cross-country skiing and snowmobiling in winter. Selkirk Shores is 3 miles west of Pulaski.

77. SALMON RIVER CANOE TRIP, Altmar to Selkirk Shores

This canoe trip of 14 miles starts at the bridge on Bridge Street in Altmar, home of the NYS Salmon River Fish Hatchery, and follows the Salmon River to the take-out point at the boat launch at Selkirk Shores State Park. River conditions vary from calm water to Class III white water at Pulaski. Water depth and flow may change suddenly with Niagara Mohawk Power dam releases. To get release times, call NIMO at 315-298-6531. There are other access points along this route.

78. SALMON RIVER FISH HATCHERY BICYCLE LOOP TOUR
Altmar to Port Ontario; 315-646-1000

The highest point on the Salmon Hatchery loop is 500' higher than Lake Ontario at the junction of Tubbs Road and County Road 22. Here, on the shoulder of the wooded Tug Hill Plateau, a panorama of the Lake Ontario shore spreads west as far as Oswego. Several public fishing access points are located on the loop's southern edge. The NYS Salmon River Fish Hatchery located just north of Altmar is a special point of interest, particularly during the March and September spawning runs. Riders will also enjoy the opportunity to stop in the lovely village of Pulaski.

To reconnect with the Seaway Trail (NYS Route 3) follow State Route 13 or County Route 5. The Salmon River Fish Hatchery Bicycle Loop tour is one of six loops in the eight-piece *Seaway Trail Bicycling* guidebook packet available from Seaway Trail, Inc., P.O. Box 660, Sackets Harbor, NY 13685; 1-800-SEAWAY-T, 315-646-1000.

Please call ahead to verify days and times of operations & events

79. SALMON RIVER FISH HATCHERY
Co. Rt. 22, Altmar; 315-298-5051

This high-tech hatchery managed by the NYS Department of Environmental Conservation produces 3.5 million coho, chinook, and landlocked Atlantic salmon, steelhead and brown trout annually for stocking in Lakes Erie, Ontario and Champlain and their tributaries. Stocking was made necessary by the destruction of habitat, overfishing, predation by an exotic parasitic fish called the sea lamprey, and numerous dams which prevented salmon from reaching spawning streams. Thanks to the work done here sportfishing opportunities in Seaway Trail waters are among the best in the world. Self-guided tours are available March to November; call for days and times.

80. DEER CREEK MARSH WILDLIFE MANAGEMENT AREA
NYS Route 3, Port Ontario; 607-753-3095

This large wildlife area of about 1200 acres has a great variety of habitats including wetlands, woodlands, open fields, and sand dunes. The State of New York purchased this parcel of land mainly to protect threatened wildlife habitats and to preserve the approximately one mile of barrier beach and sand dune shoreline. Deer Creek is an ideal place to observe wetland plants and animals from a canoe. Birdwatching and nature study are permitted in the area but camping, picnicking, swimming, and snowmobiling are prohibited.

81. SANDY POND BEACH UNIQUE AREA, Sandy Pond, 716-546-8030

This area is a biological and recreational treasure. Its white sand beaches have attracted visitors from near and far for generations. The rolling dunes are part of a 17-mile barrier system unique in New York. The dunes, sand flats, and pond-side wetlands provide rich habitats that attract concentrations of migrating and breeding birds. The Nature Conservancy, in cooperation with the NYS Department of Environmental Conservation and The Friends of Sandy Pond Beach, manages a natural area covering nearly a mile of Lake Ontario sandy beach for public enjoyment. To cross the spit from pond shore to lake shore, two special areas are provided. Please respect adjacent privately-owned lands. Visitors are welcome from one half hour before sunrise to one half hour after sunset. Camping, open campfires, vehicles and glass are prohibited; self-contained heaters are allowed. Dogs must be kept on a leash.

Please call ahead to verify days and times of operations & events

JEFFERSON COUNTY, NYS' SEAWAY TRAIL

82. LAKEVIEW WILDLIFE MANAGEMENT AREA
Route 3, Ellisburg

This is a 3461-acre wildlife area along the shoreline of Lake Ontario managed by the NYS Department of Environmental Conservation (DEC). In general, permissible public use of wildlife management areas includes hunting, fishing, trapping, wildlife observation and photography, conservation education, hiking, snowshoeing, and cross-country skiing. Activities generally prohibited are any use of motor vehicles, overnight mooring or storage of boats, camping, swimming, skiing (other than cross-country), picnicking, and mechanized boating. Wildlife-oriented activities are encouraged within this framework.

If there are questions about a particular area the appropriate regional DEC office should be consulted. At Lakeview, hunting of deer, grouse, pheasant, rabbit, and waterfowl is permitted in season and pursuant to DEC regulations.

An outstanding feature of this area is that it includes almost five miles of barrier beaches and sand dunes. The dunes are fragile ecosystems and with the barrier beaches they protect the inland wetland from damage by wave erosion. Both dune and wetland ecosystems contain many rare and unusual plant and animal species. The wildlife area is bordered on the north by Southwick Beach State Park.

83. SOUTH COLWELL POND CANOE TRIP
Route 3 to Montario Point Road

The starting point for this canoe trip can be either the parking lot and boat launch on Colwell Pond or Lakeview Pond. These two ponds on the south and north ends respectively of Lakeview Wildlife Management Area are connected by ponds and streams inside the barrier beach system. Heavy growth of aquatic vegetation during summer may limit the distance the canoer will be able to paddle.

Keep a sharp eye for wild morning glories on the pond banks, water lilies, herons and other waterfowl.

Please call ahead to verify days and times of operations & events

84. SOUTHWICK BEACH STATE PARK, NYS Route 3, Woodville; 315-846-5338, Reservations: 800-456-CAMP; off-season: 315-938-5083

Southwick Beach is a 682-acre state park with a natural sandy swimming beach that extends almost the entire length of the facility, with a modern bathhouse. The park has 112 campsites and 44 trailer sites with electricity. Other features are picnic areas with tables and grills, a boat launching ramp, and concession stand.

The Filmore Brook/Lake Ontario Dune Trail here is more than a mile long with an illustrated interpretive guide available at the park entrance gate. In the shore area the trail has a dune walkover bridge to protect the delicate dune ecosystem. A branch of the trail leads to Lakeview Pond on the north end of the Lakeview Wildlife Management Area. Some plants and trees to watch for include beach grass, wild grape vines, jack-in-the-pulpit, marsh fern, marsh marigold, poison ivy, black cherry and green ash trees, Christmas fern, beech, cedar and maple trees, jewelweed and wild raspberry. Bird and animal life often seen includes northern leopard and bull frogs, painted and snapping turtles, wood thrush, great blue heron, marsh wren, and least bittern. You may even catch a glimpse of a red fox or white-tailed deer. Visitors are requested to stay on trails and off the dunes.

Southwick Beach is open for camping and swimming mid-May to mid-October. Winter activities include cross-country skiing, and snowshoeing.

85. EL DORADO BEACH PRESERVE, NYS Route 3, Henderson Harbor

To get to the preserve from the Seaway Trail, take Stony Creek Road west to the first left turn and watch for El Dorado Beach Preserve sign. This 360-acre preserve is owned and operated by The Nature Conservancy (see #12).

Located on a major flyway between James Bay and Atlantic coastal marshes of the United States, it has one of the largest and most diverse concentrations of fall migrant shorebirds in upstate New York. The northern three-fourths of the property is underlain by limestone bedrock that projects into the lake forming outcrops and pools. These provide gulls, terns, and shorebirds with perches for resting and feeding.

Please call ahead to verify days and times of operations & events

85. El Dorado Beach Preserve (con't)

The southern quarter of the property has a broad, sandy beach and some of the best high sand dune communities on the shores of Lake Ontario. The preserve is open to the public for nature study and birdwatching. To avoid damaging these fragile ecosystems, visitors are requested to stay off the sand dunes. To minimize human disturbance and provide the best possible view of birds for everyone, stay on the trail and use the birdviewing blind. The preserve manager is often present during summer months to provide suggestions for visitors.

86. Westcott Beach State Park, NYS Route 3,
Sackets Harbor, NY 13685; 315-938-5083,
Reservations: 800-456-CAMP

Westcott Beach is a state park of 318 acres with 2000' of Lake Ontario shoreline. The park actually faces Henderson Bay, thus its waters are protected from the strong winds and waves common on unsheltered lake shores. Wescott Beach has 168 campsites (85 electric), six miles of hiking trails, picnic areas with tables, a playground and playing fields, a concession stand, and a boat launching ramp with dockage. The park is open year'round but is available for camping only mid-May through mid-October. It is a popular ice fishing location.

87. Sackets Harbor Bicycle Loop Tour
Sackets Harbor; 315-646-1000

The Sackets Harbor Bicycle Loop tour runs parallel to the Black River between Dexter and Brownville. The river enters a narrow canyon, in places up to 200' deep, near Dexer. The resulting stretch of white water is a favorite with rafters and kayakers. The ride's terrain is generally level through farmland and fertile lowlands with a few short hills. West of Sulphur Springs, herons nest near Mill Creek. Stop a while in the village of Sackets Harbor for a picnic at the State Historic Battlefield Site on the lakeshore; in Brownville, visit the Jacob Brown Mansion. Some heavy traffic may be encountered along some stretches. This tour is one of six in the *Seaway Trail Bicycling* guidebook packet with maps, write: Seaway Trail, Inc., P.O. Box 660, Sackets Harbor, NY 13685; 1-800-SEAWAY-T, 315-646-1000.

Please call ahead to verify days and times of operations & events

88. THOMPSON PARK ZOO
Thompson Park, off State St., Watertown; 315-782-6180

A panoramic view of the City of Watertown and the surrounding countryside is seen from Thompson Park. This 355-acre Frederick Law Olmsted-designed park is home to Thompson Park Zoo, a creative playground, and exercise trails. A recent renovation of the zoo now provides natural habitats showcasing flora and fauna native to Northern New York and northeastern North America such as elk, bears, wolves, owls of the Tug Hill Plateau, lynx of the Adirondacks, and turtles of the St. Lawrence River region. Special seasonal highlights are the children's petting zoo with pony and camel rides; and the butterfly garden. Programming and events are offered year'round. There is an admission fee. Hours are 10 am - 5 pm daily; closed Thanksgiving and Christmas.

89. SCI-TECH CENTER OF NORTHERN NEW YORK
155 Arsenal St., Watertown; 315-788-1340

This hands-on museum, handicapped accessible, stimulates an interest in science with exhibits including a sand pendulum, laser, binary number machine, and garden of smells. Admission is charged.

90. DEXTER MARSH WILDLIFE MANAGEMENT AREA
NYS Route 180,   Baggs Corner

Dexter Marsh Wildlife Area is 1339 acres managed by the NYS Department of Environmental Conservation. Waterfowl hunting is permitted in season and in compliance with appropriate state laws. For information on wildlife management areas, see #82.

91. LONG POINT STATE PARK, State Park Road, Point Peninsula;
315-649-5258, Reservations: 800-456-CAMP;
off-season: 315-938-5083

Long Point, on the north shore of Point Peninsula, faces Chaumont Bay on Lake Ontario. From the Seaway Trail (NYS Route 12E), take North Shore Road to State Park Road and watch for the Long Point State Park sign. This remote area is almost completely surrounded by water with great views from every campsite. Features include 88 campsites (18 electric), a boat launching ramp, dockage, and a playground. The park is open for camping mid-May-early September, and is popular for ice fishing.

Please call ahead to verify days and times of operations & events

92. CHAUMONT BARRENS, VanAlstyne Road, Chaumont: 716-546-8030

The Chaumont Barrens is a unique area managed by The Nature Conservancy, an organization whose mission is to global preservation of natural diversity. The Barrens is a unique alvar landscape unlike any other natural area in the northeastern United States. Swedish scientists coined the term "alvar" to describe similar barrens in their country. Characterized by a mosaic of austere, windswept vegetation, North American alvar sites lie scattered along an arc from northwestern Jefferson County through Ontario to northern Michigan. Many scientists think that during the retreat of the last glacier some 10,000 years ago a huge ice dam burst. A torrent of unimaginable proportions swept away all surface debris and dissolved limestone bedrock along cracks and fissures. The result, a strikingly linear pattern of vegetation visible on aerial photographs, attracted The Nature Conservancy's interest and they discovered the best-preserved of a handful of New York alvar sites.

Alvar communities are supported by a rare combination of extreme conditions: shallow soil, flooding, and drought, which provide habitat for a unique mixture of plants, including many rare in New York State. The vegetation mosaic includes exposed outcrops, deep fissures, and rubbly moss gardens as well as patches of woods, shrub savannas, and open grasslands. Visit in April to see early saxifrage, May for balsam ragwort, June - early buttercup and prairie smoke, July - most plants in droop in the heat, August- prairie grasses and early goldenrod, and September - upland white aster. Listen and watch for the prairie warbler, red-tailed hawk, northern goshawk, Cooper's hawk, sharp-shinned hawk and American kestrel among other birds.

The Chaumont Barrens are open during daylight hours from early May until mid-fall depending upon flooding season. Visitors are asked to use the trails and stepping stones provided on the two-mile trail. Summer heat may call for you to carry drinking water. Pets, vehicles and bicycles are not allowed. No collecting of plants, animals, or rocks is allowed. The Nature Conservancy asks that you "leave only footprints and take only pictures." The information provided here was taken from the Conservancy's Chaumont Barrens interpretive brochure.

Please call ahead to verify days and times of operations & events

93. CAPE VINCENT FISHERIES STATION
Broadway St., Cape Vincent; 315-654-2147

This facility is the base for the Lake Ontario-St. Lawrence River Field Unit of the Great Lakes Fisheries Section. Until recently the basic purpose of the dock area was for fisheries units use only. It is available now for limited public use on a first-come basis. Boaters may use the facility for up to two overnight dockings in any week. Water can be supplied to boaters for drinking and the station toilet facilities are open 8 am to 5 pm daily. The station maintains an aquarium in which many of the game fish and others in the region can be viewed. Call for open hours.

94. CAPE VINCENT BICYCLE LOOP TOUR
Cape Vincent; 315-646-1000

Bicyclists will enjoy a pleasant, level ride around the Cape Vincent Peninsula through open country. Jackets may be required as it can be windy. Summer brings fields of multi-colored wildflowers near Rosiere. Ashland Road passes through the bird refuge at Ashland Flats Wildlife Area. The lightkeeper's house at Tibbetts Points Lighthouse is now a hostel. This tour is one of six in the *Seaway Trail Bicycling* guidebook packet available from Seaway Trail, Inc., P.O. Box 660, Sackets Harbor, NY 13685; 1-800-SEAWAY-T, 315-646-1000.

95. BURNHAM POINT STATE PARK, NYS Route 12E, Cape Vincent;
315-654-2324, Reservations: 800-456-CAMP, off-season: 315-654-2522

Burnham Point is a small, quiet, lightly wooded park on the St. Lawrence River. It is ideal for boating, fishing and relaxing. The park has 52 campsites (16 electric), picnic areas, a playground, swimming beach, and a boat dock with several slips and a launch ramp.

96. CEDAR POINT STATE PARK, NYS Route 12E, Clayton;
315-686-2522, Reservations: 800-456-CAMP

This is a park of about 46 acres with 2760' of shoreline along the St. Lawrence River. Facilities include 172 campsites (33 full hookups), picnic areas, swimming beaches with bathhouse, playground, playing fields, and marina with boat slips and launch ramp. The park

Please call ahead to verify days and times of operations & events

96. Cedar Point State Park (con't)

is an excellent place for fishing, boating, and swimming. Visitors come to relax, enjoy the beautiful scenery, and watch the freighter traffic on the St. Lawrence River. Throughout the summer there are special events featuring folk singers, puppet shows, storytellers, and other performers. Winter activities include ice fishing and skiing. The park is open for camping from early May through Columbus Day.

97. Thousand Island Tours

Clayton and Alexandria Bay; 315-482-2520, 800-8-ISLAND

Although it is called "Thousand" Islands, this region of the St. Lawrence River actually contains 1864 islands. These vary greatly in size from several thousand acres to others only large enough to support a single tree. To be designated an island in this region there must be enough land above water to support some grass and a tree. In the absence of these characteristics the island becomes a shoal. The islands are of great beauty and historic interest. Luncheon cruises, dinner cruises, romantic twilight cruises or plain sightseeing tours can be scheduled daily in season in Clayton and Alexandria Bay.

98. Grass Point State Park, NYS Route 12E, Clayton;
315-686-4472/654-2522, Reservations: 800-456-CAMP

Skirmishes of the French and Indian War, the Revolutionary War, the War of 1812, and the Patriots War of 1837 took place near Grass Point State Park. The park offers panoramic views of the American shipping channel of the St. Lawrence River, Rock Island Lighthouse (a National Historic Register site and New York State Park), and many islands in the area. Boaters enjoy the park because of the 32 slips available and its close proximity to good fishing.

There are state-owned islands with public docking and other interesting spots scattered for miles up and down the river which make for enjoyable boating. Other facilities at Grass Point include 78 campsites (17 with electricity), picnic areas, a playground, swimming beach with bathhouse, a boat launching ramp.

The park is open for camping mid-May to early September. Winter activities are ice fishing, cross-country skiing, and snowmobiling.

Please call ahead to verify days and times of operations & events

99. WELLESLEY ISLAND STATE PARK, Wellesley Island, Fineview; 315-482-2722, Reservations: 800-456-CAMP

This 2636-acre park is off Route I-81 on an island in American waters of the St. Lawrence River. In 1906 the park was an operating farm owned by Edison Bradly, owner of The Old Grand Dad Distillery. Mr. Bradly engaged in a major reforestation project, planting hundreds of forest trees, fruit trees, berry fields, and grape arbors. Remnants of some of these can still be seen today. The park was purchased in the early 1950s by the Thousand Island Park Commission and opened to the public in 1954. Since then the park has grown into a small city with 10 winterized cabins and 430 campsites (57 with full hookups), picnic areas, a 9-hole golf course, swimming beach, four boat launching ramps, and a marina with 90 slips. Winter activities include cross-country skiing.

100. MINNA ANTHONY COMMON NATURE CENTER
Wellesley Island State Park, Wellesley Island; 315-482-2479

This 600-acre nature center was named for an early Wellesley Island conservationist. The museum here features live collections of fish, reptiles, and amphibians; an observation beehive complete with live bees; mounted waterfowl and birds of prey; decoys, geological specimens, wildflowers; and much more.

Bordered by the St. Lawrence River, the center contains a variety of wildlife habitats. Eight miles of trails and walkways crisscross the center, one of which is specially marked for the blind and visually- impaired. For the winter months programming at the center includes the use of seven miles of groomed trails for cross-country skiing and snowshoeing. The Center is located in Wellesley Island State Park (see #99).

101. WATERSON POINT STATE PARK
Fineview; 315-482-2272

Accessible only by boat, Waterson Point State Park has the distinction of being one of the first state parks in the Thousand Islands area. It is a favorite site for shore dinners for the guides and fishermen who make a catch in nearby Lost Channel.

Please call ahead to verify days and times of operations & events

102. DeWolf Point State Park, Cross Island Rd, Fineview;
315-482-2722, 800-456-CAMP

This park is located on Lake of the Isles just off Route I-81. It is operated as part of Wellesley Island State Park. DeWolf Point is a quiet and scenic park with 14 cabins and 12 campsites. A recently developed boat launching ramp provides public access to the Lake of the Isles. This is a popular ice fishing location.

103. Canoe Point & Picñic Point State Parks
Grindstone Island; 315-686-4472;
Reservations: 800-456-CAMP

Both of these parks are located on the northeastern end of Grindstone Island facing Eel Bay and the Canadian Channel. Grindstone Island is the fourth largest of the Thousand Islands and is accessible by boat only. Canoe Point is a state park of 70 partially developed acres with five cabins and 35 non-electric campsites. There are also picnic areas, shelters, rest rooms, and dock space for several boats. It is open for camping mid-May to just after Labor Day.

Picnic Point is located just south of Canoe Point and is available for boating day use only. It is an ideal spot for picnics and relaxation. The closest boat access for both parks is from Wellesley Island State Park or Grass Point State Park.

104. Rock Island State Park, Fishers Landing; 315-654-2522

Rock Island Lighthouse is an historic landmark located in the American Channel offshore from Fishers Landing. It is a four-acre park accessible only by boat. The lighthouse is not open to the public but this is an excellent site for picnicking and watching the freighter traffic on the St. Lawrence Seaway. There are no restroom facilities on the island. The park with its dock space for about five boats is open May through September.

105. Mary Island State Park, off Wellesley Island; 315-654-2522,
Reservations: 800-456-CAMP

Mary Island is a 13-acre state park accessible only by boat at the eastern end of Wellesley Island. The park has 12 secluded waterfront

Please call ahead to verify days and times of operations & events

campsites, picnic areas with tables and grills, hiking trails and three boat docks.

The park is available for both campers and day use visitors mid-May through Labor Day. The closest boating access to the park is from Keewaydin State Park (see #106) or Kring Point State Park (see #107).

106. KEEWAYDIN STATE PARK, NYS Route 12, Alexandria Bay; 315-482-3331, Reservations: 800-456-CAMP

A park of 179 acres, Keewaydin is the Thousand Islands Regional Headquarters for the NYS Office of Parks, Recreation, and Historic Preservation. Facilities at the park include 41 campsites (no utilities), a picnic area with tables and fireplaces, a large swimming pool and bathhouse, and a marina with boat launching ramp and 70 boat slips.

Many people like to watch the ocean-going vessels as they pass through the American Narrows section of the St. Lawrence Seaway just offshore of the park. The campground is open mid-May through Labor Day and the marina from mid-May to mid-October.

The park is open year'round with winter activities of ice skating, ice fishing, and cross-country skiing.

107. KRING POINT STATE PARK, NYS Route 12, Redwood; 315-482-2444, Reservations: 800-456-CAMP

This 56-acre park is unique in that it is a narrow peninsula of land with the south shore facing Goose Bay and the north shore facing the St. Lawrence River. From every campsite visitors can watch ships from all over the world navigate the St. Lawrence Seaway. A great variety of bird life can be seen on the shore of the park and on the surrounding islands. There are 100 campsites (29 electric), eight cabins, picnic areas with shelters, a swimming beach, a recreation building, two boat launching ramps, and two boat docks.

The park is open from the first Saturday in May to Columbus Day. In winter, visitors enjoy ice fishing and cross-country skiing.

Please call ahead to verify days and times of operations & events

108. INDIAN RIVER WILDLIFE MANAGEMENT AREA
English Settlement Road, Chapel Corners

This is a 968-acre wildlife area about six miles south of the Seaway Trail, managed by the NYS Department of Environmental Conservation (DEC). The hunting of turkeys, grouse, and hare is permitted in season and in keeping with DEC rules and regulations. For information on NYS Wildlife Management Areas see #82.

109. IRONSIDES ISLAND PRESERVE, Township of Alexandria

Located in the St. Lawrence River on the Jefferson County-St. Lawrence County line, Ironsides Island is a 20-acre preserve owned by The Nature Conservancy (see entry #12). The island is oblong in shape with 30-40' cliffs rising out of the water along each side. A rust-colored lichen growing on those cliffs gives the island its name.

The island was purchased in 1965 by the Conservancy to preserve one of the largest nesting colonies of great blue herons in New York State. More than 500 nests have been counted in the tops of white pines, red maples, red oaks, and white ashes that grow on the island. Ironsides Island has been designated a National Natural Landmark and has been given legal protection by NYS. A 1979 law prohibits trespass on the island during the heron's nesting period from April 1 to August 1 each year. Visitors to the island must obtain written permission from The Nature Conservancy - Central New York Chapter, Box 175, Ithaca, NY 14851. After obtaining permission the best approach to the island is to use the boat launching ramp at Kring Point State Park (see #107) and travel down the river for 1.5 miles.

Please call ahead to verify days and times of operations & events

110. CEDAR ISLAND STATE PARK, Chippewa Bay;
315-654-2522, Reservations: 800-456-CAMP

Cedar Island is a state park of 10 acres accessible only by boat. It has dock space for about 10 boats. The park occupies about half of the island and has 12 lightly wooded campsites. The other half of the island is privately owned. The park is also available for day use with picnic areas, restrooms, and a picnic pavilion that can accommodate a party of up to 18 people. A hiking trail along the eastern side of the park offers an opportunity to study local wildlife and a superb view of Chippewa Bay and surrounding islands. The nearest approach to the park is to use the boat launching facilities at the village of Chippewa Bay. The park is open mid-May to Labor Day.

111. BLACK CREEK BICYCLE LOOP TOUR
NYS Route 12, Chippewa Bay; 315-646-1000

The Black Creek Bicycle Loop tour, one of six included in the eight-piece *Seaway Trail Bicycling* guidebook packet, follows quiet backroads through forest and farmland. Riders travel through South Hammond State Forest, a small tract of forests and open meadows near the village of South Hammond, and cross back and forth over Black Creek, a broad, slow-moving stream filled with cattails and water lilies. This is one of six loop tours found in the *Seaway Trail Bicycling* guidebook packet available from Seaway Trail, Inc., P.O. Box 660, Sackets Harbor, NY 13685; 1-800-SEAWAY-T, 315-646-1000.

112. JACQUES CARTIER STATE PARK, NYS Route 12, Ogdensburg;
315-375-6371

Jacques Cartier is a 463-acre park with 2500' of shoreline located 11 miles west of the City of Ogdensburg. The two biggest draws for the park are the unlimited opportunities for boating and the excellent fishing. The park is located on the St. Lawrence River in a well-protected bay for boat docking with a sandy beach for swimming.

Please call ahead to verify days and times of operations & events

112. JACQUES CARTIER STATE PARK (CON'T)

The park also has 99 campsites (25 electric), a concession stand, picnic areas, restrooms, and a boat launching ramp. The camping season is May through Columbus Day weekend. The park is open year'round with ice fishing in winter.

113. FISH CREEK WILDLIFE MANAGEMENT AREA, Heuvelton

This is a wildlife area of 4,483 acres managed by the NYS Department of Conservation (DEC). Deer and waterfowl hunting are permitted in season and in keeping with NYS DEC rules and regulations. This large wildlife area, located 6.5 miles southwest of Heuvelton, is an excellent setting for the study of north country plants and animals. For information about NYS Wildlife Management Areas see #82.

114. ST. LAWRENCE STATE PARK, NYS Route 37, Ogdensburg; 315-393-1977

St. Lawrence Park, four miles east of the City of Ogdensburg, is a 265-acre facility with a 9-hole golf course bordering the St. Lawrence Seaway. The flat and rolling hill topography has a variety of habitats from deciduous forest to successional fields. The property is crossed by four hiking trails. The golf season is mid-April through Columbus Day weekend. The park is open year'round with sledding and cross-country skiing in winter.

115. EEL WEIR STATE PARK, NYS Route 812, Ogdensburg; 315-393-1138

To get to this park from the Seaway Trail (NYS Route 37), turn south on NYS Route 812 and follow the signs. Eel Weir is a small park with 600' of shoreline along the Oswegatchie River. The park with its 34 non-electric campsites is the perfect place to get away from it all. Features include a boat launching ramp, picnic areas, and a pavilion that can hold a group of up to 50 people. No boat dock is available but the park is ideal for canoes and rowboats. Eel Weir State Park is open Memorial Day to Labor Day and makes a pleasant stopping point for a picnic for bicyclists following the Black Lake Bicycle Loop tour, one of six published in the *Seaway Trail Bicycling* guidebook packet (see #116).

Please call ahead to verify days and times of operations & events

116. BLACK LAKE BICYCLE LOOP TOUR
Ogdensburg; 315-646-1000

The Oswegatchie River, a gently flowing, peaceful stream, runs parallel to the eastern edge of the Black Lake Bicycle Loop tour. Eel Weir State Park, located just a few miles south of Ogdensburg, offers picnic facilities. Just south of the park is Black Lake, the most northern of a chain of lakes called the Indian River Lakes. At 20 miles long, Black Lake is the largest of the Indian River Lakes, but it is also very shallow. Its many bays and excellent aquatic habitat have earned Black Lake a reputation among biologists as a "fish factory." The north end has high, steep banks and a marshy shoreline. The loop brings you back to Ogdensburg along a stretch of Route 37 which parallels the St. Lawrence River.

In Ogdensburg, the oldest settled town in St. Lawrence County, be sure to visit the Frederick Remington Museum. This tour is one of six loops found in the eight-piece Seaway Trail Bicycling guidebook packet available from Seaway Trail, Inc., P.O. Box 660, Sackets Harbor, NY 13685; 1-800-SEAWAY-T, 315-646-1000.

117. OSWEGATCHIE RIVER CANOE TRIP
Newton Falls-Ogdensburg

From Newton Falls near Cranberry Lake to the St. Lawrence River at Ogdensburg, the Oswegatchie River offers 100 miles of excellent fishing and canoeing. For a detailed description of this canoe trip, write: St. Lawrence County Chamber of Commerce, Drawer A, Canton, NY 13617; 315-386-4000.

118. UPPER AND LOWER LAKES WILDLIFE MANAGEMENT AREA
Rensselaer Falls

This is an 8,782-acre wildlife area managed by the NYS Department of Environmental Conservation (DEC). Hunting of deer, pheasant, and waterfowl is permitted in season and in compliance with DEC rules and regulations. For information about NYS DEC Wildlife Management Areas see #82.

Please call ahead to verify days and times of operations & events

119. INDIAN CREEK NATURE CENTER, Renssalaer Falls

The nature center is located in the Upper and Lower Lakes Wildlife Management Area, one mile east of Rensselaer Falls (see entry #118). To get to the center from the Seaway Trail, take NYS Route 68 south from Ogdensburg to County Route 14 four miles north of Canton. Turn right (west) on Route 14 and look for the entrance to Indian Creek Nature Center on the left. The center has a learning center, observation tower and blinds, and several trails including many miles of walking paths, a wildflower loop, succession and lowland trails, and a trail of about one-half mile for the handicapped. For a small fee an excellent, illustrated guide is available to give the visitor a self-guided introduction to north country plants and animals.

120. COLES CREEK STATE PARK
NYS Route 37, Waddington; 315-388-5636

The New York Power Authority constructed this park during the development of the St. Lawrence-FDR Power Project in the late 1950s. It is located on a section of the St. Lawrence River called Lake St. Lawrence, a body of water 25 miles long and four miles wide that was formed by the Robert Moses Power Dam. This is a large park of 1200 acres with 235 campsites (154 electric). These sites are in both wooded and open areas and many of them offer a view of the river. Other park features includes picnic areas, a swimming beach, playground, boat launching ramp, and Coles Creek Park Marina. The park is a good place to relax and enjoy the fauna and flora of the north country. Camping season is mid-May through Labor Day.

121. GRASS RIVER CANOE TRIP

From Degrasse to the St. Lawrence River, the Grass River offers approximately 85 miles of fishing and canoeing. The upstream section from Degrasse to Pyrites is a cold water river supporting brown trout and brook trout. The downstream section from Pyrites to the St. Lawrence has warm water species such as walleye and northern pike. For a booklet with a complete description of this canoe trip, write: St. Lawrence County Chamber of Commerce, Drawer A, Canton, NY 13617; 315-386-4000.

Please call ahead to verify days and times of operations & events

122. WILSON HILL WILDLIFE MANAGEMENT AREA
NYS Route 37, Massena

Wilson Hill is a wildlife area of 3,526 acres managed by the NYS Department of Environmental Conservation (DEC). Hunting of deer, grouse, pheasant, rabbit, hare, and waterfowl is permitted in season and in compliance with DEC rules and regulations. To get to the area from the Seaway Trail (NYS Route 37), take NYS Route 131 north to Willard Road, then turn left and watch for the parking lot on the left. Wilson Hill Wildlife Management Area has two trails: a nature trail that leads to an observation tower overlooking the refuge, and a 1.6 mile hiking trail.

The hiking trail doubles as a cross-country ski trail during winter. Bicyclists following the Wilson Hill Bicycle Loop tour from the *Seaway Trail Bicycling* guidebook packet (see entry #123) will especially enjoy the opportunity to see spring and fall bird migrations in this area. For more information on NYS Wildlife Management Areas see #82.

123. WILSON HILL BICYCLE LOOP TOUR, Louisville; 315-646-1000

The hardwood forests lining the banks of the Grass and Raquette Rivers are home to numerous animals, including deer, fox, mink, bobcat, otter, weasel, and an occasional black bear. Spring and fall bird migrations use both rivers and the nearby Wilson Hill Wildlife Management Area (see #122). At Wilson Hill you might see herons, loons, owls, hawks, and possibly a bald eagle. This bicycle ride is mildly challenging, crossing the Raquette River using an old steel bridge now closed to motorists. Walk your bike over the bridge's coarse, steel-grate surface. Just upstream the river drops over a small dam. There are several rolling hills and short, steep grades to peddle near Louisville on County Road 69. The railroad overpass on Tiernon Ridge Road is also surfaced with steel grating and requires caution.

The *Seaway Trail Bicycling* guidebook packet offers this loop tour and five others with maps, an 111-page guidebook, and fold-out maps brochure in a plastic bag for bicycling the eastern half of NYS' Seaway Trail. Write or call: Seaway Trail, Inc., P.O. Box 660, Sackets Harbor, NY 13685; 1-800-SEAWAY-T, 315-646-1000.

Please call ahead to verify days and times of operations & events

124. RAQUETTE RIVER CANOE TRIP
Piercefield to the St. Lawrence River

From Piercefield to the St. Lawrence River, the Raquette River, a NYS-designated Scenic River, offers about 87 miles of everything from white water canoeing to paddling on reservoirs. A convenient feature of the river is that most of it is readily accessible by motor vehicle. This makes it easy for a family or an individual to enjoy a favorite stretch of the river at any time.

Bicyclists on the Wilson Hill Bicycle Loop tour (see #123) cross over and back along a short stretch of the Raquette River, nicknamed the "Workhorse River of the North." Its waters drop some 1,400 vertical feet from the river's headwaters until they flow quietly into the St. Lawrence River near Massena to provide hydroelectric power. For a booklet detailing the trip, write: St. Lawrence Chamber of Commerce, Drawer A, Canton, NY 13617; 315-386-4000.

125. ROBERT MOSES STATE PARK
off Rte. 37, Massena; 315-769-8663

This park of 2,322 acres is the second largest state park in the Thousand Islands region. Located on both the mainland and on Barnhart Island, it is reached by a tunnel under the Eisenhower Lock of the St. Lawrence Seaway. The park has 169 campsites (28 electric), 15 cabins, picnic areas, playgrounds, swimming area, and a 42-slip marina. The Robert Moses Nature Center, located in the park, has a nature museum and it offers the visitor an opportunity to observe the local fauna and flora on its several nature trails. The nature center also has cross-country skiing trails for winter recreation.

126. ST. LAWRENCE-FDR POWER PROJECT VISITORS CENTER
Rte. 131, Barnhart Island, Massena; 315-764-0226,
800-262-NYPA in NYS

This center, operated by the New York Power Authority, is set amidst some of New York's finest wilderness recreation lands. Displays offer hands-on exhibits, a bicycle generator to ride, and visual terrain and relief maps of the local landscape. Two Thomas Hart Benton wall murals depict early regional exploration and Indian-European encounters. Hike, camp, boat and fish at neighboring Robert Moses State Park (see #125). Admission and parking are free.

Please call ahead to verify days and times of operations & events

127. St. Lawrence Aquarium & Ecological Center
Robinsons Bay, Massena; 315-769-0787

The St. Lawrence Aquarium & Ecological Center, in development at the time of writing, will be a marvelous showpiece for the St. Lawrence County segment of NYS' Seaway Trail. Situated on approximately 150 acres of mixed deciduous forest, low wetland area, and second-growth scrub woodland, the center on the south channel of the St. Lawrence River at Robinsons Bay will have a rustic north country design. It will be dedicated to education, research and interpretation relating to freshwater environment and ecology, particularly oriented to the challenges of the St. Lawrence River Valley and watershed, including the Great Lakes and Adirondack Mountains.

Exhibits will provide natural habitat conditions for aquatic and terrestrial plants and animals, including those of puddles, bogs, marshes, ponds, streams, rivers and lakes. Some specific species which may be seen are birch, aspen and hemlock trees; trout, muskellunge, salmon, and walleye; common mergansers and loons; muskrats and painted turtles. An exhibit of river otters is sure to be a lively highlight for visitors.

The water in the river at Robinsons Bay is free of major organic pollutants and sufficient in dissolved oxygen for operation of the facility. Particulate filtration will make waters clearer for viewing of the outside stream exhibits, indoor pavilion displays, and research area projects. Classrooms, a theatre, gift and book shop, and research library are planned elements of this exciting new project scheduled to open in 1998.

river otter

Please call ahead to verify days and times of operations & events

A SEAWAY TRAIL BIRDER'S CHECKLIST

The following species and numbers of birds were seen during the most recent National Audubon Society's Christmas Bird Counts for the Seaway Trail region. Counts were taken in the vicinities of Jamestown, Fredonia, East Aurora, Oak Orchard Swamp, Rochester, Central Cayuga County, Oswego-Fulton, Watertown, and Massena. The information was provided by the National Audubon Society, 700 Broadway, New York, NY 10003.

Eastern Bluebird - 62
Red-winged Blackbird - 319
Rusty Blackbird - 4
Bufflehead - 915
Northern Cardinal - 1173
Gray Catbird - 4
Black-capped Chickadee - 4824
American Coot - 949
Double-crested Cormorant - 17
Brown-headed Cowbird - 323
Brown Creeper - 71
Red Crossbill - 13
White-winged Crossbill - 64
American Crow - 13,525
Rock Dove - 6409
Mourning Dove - 3260
American Black Duck - 1791
Canvasback Duck - 2829
Redhead Duck - 69
Ring-necked Duck - 6
Wood Duck - 23
Bald Eagle - 3
Common Eider - 1
Peregrine Falcon - 2
House Finch - 5953
Purple Finch - 44
Northern Flicker - 175

Northern Fulmar - 1
Gadwall - 80
Barrow's Goldeneye - 1
Common Goldeneye - 4320
American Goldfinch - 1085
Canada Goose - 35,282
Snow Goose - 2
Northern Goshawk - 1
Common Grackle - 6
Pied-billed Grebe - 13
Horned Grebe - 30
Red-necked Grebe - 4
Evening Grosbeak - 81
Pine Grosbeak - 20
Ruffed Grouse - 19
Bonaparte's Gull - 4850
Glaucous Gull - 10
Herring Gull - 7835
Iceland Gull - 9
Great Black-backed Gull - 2924
Lesser Black-backed Gull - 1
Little Gull - 1
Ring-billed Gull - 20,873
Gyrfalcon - 1
Northern Harrier - 46
Cooper's Hawk - 40
Red-shouldered Hawk - 2

Red-tailed Hawk - 448

Rough-legged Hawk - 29

Sharp-shinned Hawk - 35

Great Blue Heron - 52

Blue Jay - 2388

Dark-eyed Junco 1457

American Kestrel - 99

Killdeer - 1

Belted Kingfisher - 16

Golden-crowned Kinglet - 175

Horned Lark - 86

Lapland Longspur - 1

Common Loon - 45

Red-throated Loon - 21

Mallard - 9186

E. Meadowlark - 1

Common Merganser - 5536

Hooded Merganser - 82

Red-breasted Merganser - 200

Northern Mockingbird - 21

Red-breasted Nuthatch - 57

White-breasted Nuthatch - 479

Oldsquaw - 3333

Barred Owl - 1

Eastern Screech Owl - 65

Great Horned Owl - 70

Long-eared Owl - 7

Short-eared Owl - 2

Snowy Owl - 3

Ring-necked Pheasant - 31

Eastern Phoebe - 1

N. Pintail - 16

Common Redpoll - 530

American Robin - 3732

Yellow-bellied Sapsucker - 2

Greater Scaup - 15,262

Lesser Scaup - 75

Black Scoter - 7

Surf Scoter - 1

White-winged Scoter - 509

Northern Shoveler - 32

Northern Shrike - 10

Pine Siskin - 2

Common Snipe - 1

Snow Bunting - 682

Fox Sparrow - 1

Song Sparrow - 119

Swamp Sparrow - 11

American Tree Sparrow - 1649

House Sparrow - 7821

White-crowned Sparrow - 23

White-throated Sparrow - 264

European Starling - 42,143

Mute Swan - 10

Tundra Swan - 104

Hermit Thrush - 1

Tufted Titmouse - 190

Rufous-sided Towhee - 2

Wild Turkey - 126

Yellow-rumped Warbler - 18

Cedar Waxwing - 2521

American Wigeon - 12

Downy Woodpecker - 627

Hairy Woodpecker - 164

Pileated Woodpecker - 25

Red-bellied Woodpecker - 171

Three-toed Woodpecker - 1

Carolina Wren - 8

Winter Wren - 7

Common Yellowthroat - 1

COMMON & BOTANICAL NAMES
FOR SEAWAY TRAIL PLANTS

The following is an alphabetized list of the common names of the plants referred to in this book. Since many plants have more than one common name the botanical name for each plant is also listed. There is only one botanical name for each species. The common and botanical names are those used in the Manual of Vascular Plants of Northeastern United States and Adjacent Canada (2nd Ed.) by H. Gleason and A. Cronquist. The abbreviation spp. indicates that there are more than one species of the genus with that common name.

american elm	*Ulmus americana*
american lotus	*Nelumbo lutea*
arrow arum	*Peltandra virginica*
arrowhead	*Sagittaria spp.*
arrow-wood	*Viburnum dentatum*
ash	*Fraxinus spp.*
aspen	*Populus spp.*
balsam fir	*Abies balsamea*
basswood	*Tilia americana*
beach grass	*Ammophila breviligulata*
beach pea	*Lathyrus maritimus*
beech	*Fagus grandifolia*
beech drops	*Epifagus virginiana*
birch	*Betula spp.*
birdsfoot trefoil	*Lotus corniculatus*
black ash	*Fraxinus nigra*
blackberry	*Rubus spp.*
black-eyed Susan	*Rubeckia hirta*
black spruce	*Picea mariana*
bladder campion	*Silene vulgaris*
bloodroot	*Sanguinaria candensis*
blue beech	*Carpinus caroliniana*
blue cohosh	*Caulophyllum thalictroides*

blue-stem goldenrod	*Solidago caesia*
bog laurel	*Kalmia polifolia*
bog rosemary	*Andromeda glaucophylla*
bouncing bet	*Saponaria officinalis*
broad-leaved arrowhead	*Sagittaria latifolia*
broad-leaved cattail	*Typha latifolia*
brown knapweed	*Centaurea jacea*
buckthorn	*Rhamnus cathartica*
burdock	*Arctium minus*
butter-and-eggs	*Linaria vulgaris*
buttonbush	*Cephalanthus occidentalis*
canada anemone	*Anemone canadensis*
canada goldenrod	*Solidago canadensis*
canada violet	*Viola canadensis*
cattail	*Typha spp.*
chestnut	*Castanea dentata*
chicory	*Cichorium intybus*
choke-cherry	*Prunus virginiana*
christmas fern	*Polystichum acrosticoides*
cladophora	*Cladophora spp.*
coltsfoot	*Tussilago farfara*
common blue violet	*Viola papilionacea*
common elder	*Sambucus canadensis*
common mullein	*Verbascum thapsus*
common ragweed	*Ambrosia artemisiifolia*
corpse plant	*Monotropa uniflora*
cottonwood	*Populus spp.*
cow vetch	*Vicia cracca*
cranberry	*Vaccinium spp.*
creeping bellflower	*Campanula rapunculoides*
crown vetch	*Coronilla varia*
curly pondweed	*Potamogeton crispus*
daisy	*Chrysanthemum leucanthemum*
dandelion	*Taraxacum officinale*
doll's eyes	*Actea alba*

downy yellow violet	*Viola pubescens*
dutchman's breetches	*Dicentra cucullaria*
dwarf sumac	*Rhus copallinum*
eelgrass	*Vallisneria americana*
elm	*Ulmus spp.*
elodea	*Elodea canadensis*
enchanter's nightshade	*Circaea lutetiana*
evening primrose	*Oenothera biennis*
everlasting pea	*Lathyrus latifolia*
false lily-of-the-valley	*Maianthemum candense*
false solomon's seal	*Smilacina racemosa*
field horsetail	*Equisetum arvense*
fragrant water lily	*Nymphaea odorata*
giant bur-reed	*Spraganium eurycarpum*
giant hogweed	*Heracleum mantegazzianum*
giant ragweed	*Ambrosia trifida*
ginseng	*Panax quinquefolius*
golden larch	*Larix laricina*
goldenrod	*Solidago spp.*
grass-pink	*Calopogon tuberosus*
greater duckweed	*Spirodela polyrhiza*
greenbriar	*Smilax spp.*
ground ivy	*Glecoma hederacea*
ground pine	*Lycopouium obscurum*
heal-all	*Prunella vulgaris*
heart-leaved aster	*Aster cordifolius*
hemlock	*Tsuga canadensis*
hepatica	*Hepatica spp.*
hickory	*Carya spp.*
hobblebush	*Virbunum alnifolium*
honeysuckle	*Lonicera spp.*
hop-hornbeam	*Ostrya virginiana*
hornwort	*Ceratophyllum demersum*
horseweed	*Conyza canadensis*
horse chestnut	*Aesculus hippocastanum*

indian pipe	*Monotropa uniflora*
ironwood	*Ostrya virginiana*
jack-in-the-pulpit	*Arisaema triphyllum*
jack pine	*Pinus banksiana*
japanese knotwood	*Polygonum caspidatum*
jewelweed	*Impatiens capensis*
knapweed	*Centaurea spp.*
labrador tea	*Ledum groenlandicum*
lamb's quarters	*Chenopodium album*
larch	*Larix larcina*
large cranberry	*Vaccinium macrocarpon*
large-flowered trillium	*Trillium grandiflorum*
large-leaved aster	*Aster macrophyllus*
leatherleaf	*Chamaedaphne calyculata*
lesser duckweed	*Lemna minor*
maple-leaved viburnum	*Viburnum acerifolium*
marsh marigold	*Caltha palustris*
mayapple	*Podophyllum peltatum*
mexican bamboo	*Polygonum cuspidatum*
milkweed	*Asclepias syriaca*
mocassin flower	*Cypripedium acaule*
mosquito fern	*Azolla caroliniana*
moth mullein	*Verbascum blattaria*
mountain ash	*Sorbus americana*
mullein	*Verbascum spp.*
musclewood	*Carpinus caroliniana*
musk mallow	*Malva moschata*
nailrod	*Typha angustifolia*
narrow-leaved cattail	*Typha angustifolia*
New England aster	*Aster novae-angliae*
nodding wild rye	*Elymus spp.*
northern red oak	*Quercus rubra*
oak	*Quercus spp.*
orange day-lily	*Hemerocallis fulva*
ox-eye daisy	*Chrysanthemum leucanthemum*

pale touch-me-not	*Impatiens pallida*
partridge berry	*Mitchella repens*
phragmites	*Phragmites australis*
pickerelweed	*Pontederia cordata*
pinesap	*Monotropa hypopithys*
pipsissewa	*Chimaphila umbellata*
pitcher plant	*Sarracenia purpurea*
plantain	*Plantago spp.*
poison hemlock	*Conium maculatum*
poison ivy	*Toxicodendron radicans*
purple loosestrife	*Lythrum salicaria*
purple trillium	*Trillium erectum*
pussywillow	*Salix discolor*
Queen Anne's lace	*Daucus carota*
ragweed	*Ambrosia spp.*
red baneberry	*Actea rubra*
red maple	*Acer rubrum*
red oak	*Quercus rubra*
red osier dogwood	*Cornus sericea*
redroot pigweed	*Amaranthus retroflexus*
reed	*Phragmites australis*
rose pogonia	*Pogonia ophioglossoides*
round-leaved sundew	*Drosera roundifolia*
sand cherry	*Prunus pumila*
sand dune willow	*Salix cordata*
sassafras	*Sassafras albidum*
sea rocket	*Cakile edentula*
seaside spurge	*Euphorbia polygonifolia*
serviceberry	*Amelanchier spp.*
shepard's purse	*Capsella bursa-pastoris*
shining clubmoss	*Lycopodium lucidulum*
silverweed	*Potentilla anserina*
smooth sumac	*Rhus glabra*
snowflake	*Leucojum aestivum*
soapwort	*Saponaria officinalis*

spatterdock	*Nuphar variegata*
spatula-leaved sundew	*Drosera intermedia*
speckled alder	*Alnus incana*
spicebush	*Lindera benzoin*
sphaghnum moss	*Sphagnum spp.*
spotted knapweed	*Centaurea maculosa*
spotted touch-me-not	*Impatiens capensis*
spotted wintergreen	*Chimaphila maculata*
spring beauty	*Claytonia viginica*
squawroot	*Conopholis americana*
squirrel corn	*Dicentra canadensis*
staghorn sumac	*Rhus typhina*
star-flowered solomon's seal	*Smilacina stellata*
striped maple	*Acer pensylvanicum*
sugar maple	*Acer saccharum*
sundew	*Drosera spp.*
swamp loosestrife	*Decodon verticillatus*
tall buttercup	*Ranunculus acris*
tamarack	*Larix laricina*
teasel	*Dipsacus sylvestris*
toothwort	*Dentaria spp.*
tree clubmoss	*Lycopodium obscurum*
trailing arbutus	*Epigaea repens*
trout lily	*Erythronium americanum*
tufted vetch	*Vicia cracca*
vetch	*Vicia spp.*
walnut	*Juglans spp.*
water lily	*Nymphaea odorata*
watermeal	*Wolffia spp.*
water milfoil	*Myriophyllum spicatum*
water shield	*Brasenia schreberi*
white baneberry	*Actea alba*
white oak	*Quercus alba*
white pine	*Pinus strobus*
white snakeroot	*Eupatorium rugosum*

white spruce	*Picea glauca*
white sweet clover	*Melilotus alba*
white water lily	*Nymphaea odorata*
wild black cherry	*Prunus serotina*
wild carrot	*Daucus carota*
wild geranium	*Geranium maculatum*
wild ginger	*Asarum canadense*
wild grape	*Vitis spp.*
wild leek	*Allium tricoccum*
wild mustard	*Sinapsis arvensis*
witch hazel	*Hamamelis virginiana*
winter cress	*Barbarea vulgaris*
wintergreen	*Gaultheria procumbens*
woolly violet	*Viola sororia*
wormwood	*Artemisia campestris*
yellow birch	*Betula alleghaniensis*
yellow sweet clover	*Melilotus officinalis*
yellow day-lily	*Hemerocallis flava*

wild grape
or
Vitis spp.

SUGGESTED READINGS

1. Abramovitz, Janet N. 1996. Imperiled Waters, Impoverished Future: The Decline of Freshwater Ecosystems. Worldwatch Paper No. 128. Worldwatch Institute, Washington, D.C.

2. Barbour, Michael, G., J.H. Burke, and W. D. Pitts. 1980. Terrestrial Plant Ecology. The Benjamin/Cummings Publishing Co, Inc., Reading, MA

3. Braun, E. Lucy. 1905. Deciduous Forests of Eastern North America. Macmillan Publishing Co, Inc., New York, NY

4. Burt, William Henry. 1969. Mammals of the Great Lakes Region. The University of Michigan Press, Ann Arbor, MI

5. 1996. Climatological Summary for Oswego, New York. Northeast Regional Climate Center, Cornell University, Ithaca, NY

6. Cox, Donald D. 1985. Common Flowering Plants of the Northeast. State University of New York Press, Albany, NY

7. Cox, Donald D. 1959. Some Postglacial Forests in Central and Western New York State. New York State Museum Bulletin No. 377, Albany, NY

8. Drumm, Judith. 1963. Mastodons and Mammoths, Ice Age Elephants of New York. Educational Leaflet No. 13. New York State Museum and Science Service, Albany, NY

9. Erlich, Paul R., D.S. Dobkin and D. Wheye. 1988. The Birders Handbook. Simon and Schuster, Inc., New York, NY

10. Ernst, Charl H. and R. W. Barbour. 1972. Turtles of the United States. University Press of Kentucky, Lexington, KY

11. Forbush, Edward H. and J.B. May. 1955. A Natural History of American Birds of Eastern and Central North America. Bramhall House, Boston, MA

12. Hamilton, William J. and J.O. Whitaker, Jr. 1979. <u>Mammals of the Eastern United States 2nd Ed</u>. Comstock Publishing Associates, Ithaca, NY

13. Hausman, Leon A. 1946. <u>Fieldbook of Eastern Birds</u>. G. P. Putnam's Sons, New York, NY

14. Hough, Jack L. 1958. <u>Geology of the Great Lakes</u>. University of Illinois Press, Urbana, IL

15. Jennings, Jesse D., editor. 1983. <u>Ancient North Americans</u>. W. H. Freeman and Company, San Francisco, CA

16. Kaufman, Peter B., T.F. Carlson, P. Dayanandan, M.L. Evans, J.B. Fisher, C. Parks, and J.R. Wells. 1991. <u>Plants, Their Biology and Importance 2nd Ed</u>. Harper & Row, Philadelphia, PA

17. Kehoe, Alice Beck. 1981. <u>North American Indians, A Comprehensive Account</u>. Prentice Hall, Inc., Englewood Cliffs, NJ

18. L.R. Johnston Associates. 1989. <u>New York's Eastern Lake Ontario Sand Dunes</u>. New York State Division of Coastal Resources and Waterfront Revitalization, Albany, NY

19. Marchard, Peter J. 1987. <u>Life the Cold, An Introduction to Winter Ecology</u>. University Press of New England, Hanover, MA

20. Merritt, Joseph F. 1987. <u>Guide to Mammals of Pennsylvania</u>. University of Pittsburgh Press, Pittsburgh, PA

21. Mitsch, William J. and J.G. Gosselink. 1986. <u>Wetlands</u>. Van Nostrand Reinhold Co., New York, NY

22. Muller, Ernest H. and D. Pair. 1987. <u>Seaway Trail Rocks & Landscapes</u>. St. Lawrence-Eastern Ontario Commission, Watertown, NY

23. 1992. *New York Agriculture Statistics*. New York Agriculture Statistics Service, Albany, NY

24. 1991-92. *Small Game Hunter and Trapper Survey, Statewide Estimated Harvest*. New York State Department of Environmental Conservation, Albany, NY

25. 1991. *Deer Take by County and Town*. New York State Department of Environmental Conservation, Albany, NY

26. Olson, Jerry S. 1958. "Rates of Succession and Soil Changes on Southern Lake Michigan Dunes," The Botanical Gazette 199: 125-170

27. Palmer, E. Lawrence and H.S. Fowler. 1975. Fieldbook of Natural History 2nd Ed. McGraw-Hill, Inc., New York, NY

28. Pope Clifford H. 1967. Turtles of the United States and Canada. Alfred A. Knopf, Inc., New York, NY

29. Ranwell, D.S. 1972. Ecology of the Salt Marshes and Sand Dunes. Chapmand and Hall Ltd., London

30. Saunders, D.A. 1989. Adirondack Mammals. SUNY College of Environmental Science and Forestry, Syracuse, NY

31. Weimer, Linda et al. 1973. Our Great Lakes. University of Wisconsin Sea Grant College Program, Madison, WI

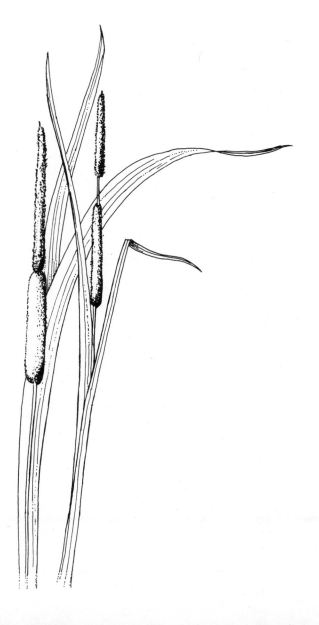

FIELD NOTES